PRAISE FOR MIKE MICHALOWICZ

THE PUMPKIN PLAN

"Michalowicz is rapidly becoming one of the most innovative business authors of our time."
    Rieva Lesonsky, former editorial director for *Entrepreneur Magazine*

"Every page, every chapter, as I read this book, I asked myself 'Michael E. Gerber, how come YOU didn't think of that?' Just remarkable. Just absolutely a remarkable book. Every one of you— entrepreneurs, business owners, read it! Do it now!"
    Michael Gerber, author of *The E-Myth*

"This book reveals degrees of knowledge and wisdom I have rarely seen in writing before. If you read only one book this year, let it be *The Pumpkin Plan*."
    Bob Burg, co-author of *The Go-Giver*

THE TOILET PAPER ENTREPRENEUR

"the business cult classic"
    BusinessWeek

"[Mike Michalowicz is] knowledgeable. He's practical. He's brilliantly, refreshingly funny."
    SmallBizTrends.com

"... if you need a swift kick in the butt to achieve your business dreams, read on."
    BrazenCareerist.com

"I can say without hesitation that *The Toilet Paper Entrepreneur*, by Mike Michalowicz is the first book my Mom ever ran off with before I even had a chance to browse it."
    Chris Brogan, social media expert and author of *The Impact Equation*

JUSTIN-
TAKE Your...

PROFIT FIRST

-Mike

**OBSIDIAN
PRESS**

PROFIT
FIRST

A SIMPLE SYSTEM TO TRANSFORM ANY BUSINESS FROM A CASH-EATING MONSTER TO A MONEY-MAKING MACHINE

MIKE MICHALOWICZ

Publisher: Obsidian Press
Print Management: Book Lab
Cover & Table Design: Liz Dobrinska
Book Design & Typesetting: Chinook Design, Inc.

2 3 4 5 6 7 8 9 10

ISBN-10: 0981808298
ISBN-13: 978-0981808291

Printed in the United States of America

CONTENTS

To my daughter, Adayla, and her piggy bank.

ACKNOWLEDGMENTS

THEY say it takes a small army to write a book. They're right. My army is Anjanette Harper.

Anjanette and I challenged each other relentlessly. We laughed. We cried. We yelled. We decided to give up, because it just couldn't be done. But finally it worked—we agreed on a small Mexican place for lunch and that the best thing to do was to share the nachos with the guacamole on the side. With that settled, we got to work on this book. Two years later we finished *Profit First*.

Thank you, Anjanette. You are the yin to my yin (yang is kinda overrated).

Thanks to Zoë Bird (who on earth knew a hyphen, en dash and em dash were different things? I take that back—you did), Nicki Harper (did you really proofread this in a barn?), Olaf Nelson (the eyeless black pig wins), Liz Dobrinska (seriously?!? Did someone just chase us down in a giant factory because your heel broke off at the welding station, thirty minutes ago, and you said nothing?), Jackie Pennetta (for booking every flight, hotel, rental car, taxi, and shipment—with never a single hiccup), Lisa DiMona (for saying "make them regret it"), and Melanie Ramiro (for helping me share everything I know, with everyone possible, on every single day available).

There was another elite force operating behind the scenes—similar to the Navy SEALS, but tougher. I called them the Fab 15. They volunteered to read Profit First the second I finished the manuscript and had eight days to read the entire book and give me critical feedback on every single concept in it. This elite team included: Debbie Horovitch (Social Sparkle & Shine), Gloria Rand (Internet Marketing Expert), Joey Himelfarb (client advocate and service provider... in other words a really, really great salesperson), Kim LaCroix (The Inspired Vacation Journal), Paula Mottshaw (Freelance Creative), Lisa Robin Young (singer and musician), Bill Walsh (father of Liam, Cecile, and Nicholas), Frank Bravata (New Millennium Technology Services), Jeff Johnson (Technology Marketing Toolkit), Jessica Oman (Write Ahead Consulting), Nicole Fende (The Numbers Whisperer), Edwin Soler (Libreria Berea), Hilary Snow (My Massage Bliss), Jason Spencer (Spencer Weddings and Entertainment) and, perhaps the most integral, kind, genuine human being on this planet, Zarik Boghossian. If you are ever in the LA area, look Zarik up. Try to grab him for a cup of coffee and some *nazook*—you will discover the secret to being a shrewd entrepreneur and the most considerate, kindhearted soul at the same time.

Thank you to all the wonderful folks at creativeLIVE. This book wouldn't exist if wasn't for you.

To my children. . . It's time for a trip to Busch Gardens (that's our Disney). To Krista, I live you.

And my thank yous would not be complete without acknowledging you. My hat's off to you, entrepreneur. You are my definition of a superhero, you know, because you are fighting to bring profitability to yourself, your family, your employees, your community and our world. Thank you for that. Keep fighting, superhero!

INTRODUCTION

Profit First = mind blown. Everything I learned about accounting is now out the door #pumpkinLIVE @MikeMichalowicz @creativeLIVE
—Kali Ann Bauer @AmbientArtPhoto

THIS book was born in San Francisco. I was at the creativeLIVE studios teaching business growth strategies from my second book, *The Pumpkin Plan*. During one of the event sessions, I explained the basic concept of the Profit First system, the simple method I developed to ensure that I would have not only a financially healthy business, but a seriously *profitable* one.

One of the tools of Profit First is the Instant Assessment, a way to quickly gauge the real financial health of your business. When I ran the assessment on a volunteer attendee, the Profit First system clicked for everyone in the room.

All creativeLIVE presentations are also broadcast live online and eight thousand viewers had tuned in for my event. Tweets and comments started flying in from all over the world. Because the Instant Assessment is so fast and easy, I wasn't totally surprised to see the many comments from online viewers saying that they had assessed their business right then and there. Entrepreneurs, CEOs, freelancers, business owners—everyone shared how relieved they were to learn this simple method. It was as though they had each experienced a sudden, total clarity, an instant jolt of confidence about the money side of their businesses.

I had shared the four core principles of Profit First and the Instant Assessment in less than thirty minutes and I saw that people didn't just understand it, they were already applying it. When a tweet came from Kali Ann Bauer @AmbientArtPhoto, I knew the Profit First system hit home. (Kali has since taken down her Twitter account, but you can check her out at AmbientArtPhotographynd.com.) Here is the tweet, captured by the creativeLIVE host:

Profit First = mind blown. Everything I learned about accounting is now out the door #pumpkinLIVE @MikeMichalowicz @creativeLIVE

But it wasn't until I met Debbie Horovitch that I understood just how vital it was that I break down the Profit First system further and make it available to entrepreneurs all over the world.

After the segment ended, we took a break. The camera and lighting people hustled to get ready for the next segment. Me? I was pumped! It was amazing to see this instant evidence showing how powerful Profit First truly is. Not only did it work for different people with different businesses of different sizes, it worked instantly. I was thrilled.

When the producer ran toward me, I threw up my hand for a high-five, but she didn't see it and went in for a fist bump instead. Then ensued the most awkward moment in human enthusiasm: when a high-five is met with a fist bump and quickly turns into a fist-five-handshake. So awkward. But she didn't even notice.

With her fist in my hand, she blurted, "That was amazing! Comments are still flying in. Can I use Profit First for my personal life? Be sure to open the next segment with a recap. Drink some water; your voice is getting a little hoarse. Take a quick five and then head over to makeup to get some shine off your forehead. And you can let go of my fist now, Mike."

The producer ran over to the lighting guys; I grabbed a glass of water, chewed on my pen and looked around to see if anyone had witnessed the fist-five.

That's when Debbie Horovitch, the entrepreneur behind the Social, Sparkle & Shine Agency—a Toronto, California firm that specializes in social media services—approached me. Debbie said, "Could we put my business through the assessment?"

"Sure," I said. "It only takes a minute or two."

Pen in my mouth, people hustling and bustling all around us, I ran through it right then and there. It was as if Debbie and I were in a world of our own. I scrawled her annual revenue number on the board. We ran the percentages. Debbie looked at the results and started to shake with sobs.

She couldn't bear to look at where she was, or where the Instant Assessment said she should be.

"I've been a fool," she said, tears streaming down her face. "Everything I have done over the last ten years is wrong. I am such a fool. I am a fool. I am a fool."

Let me admit right now, I'm a co-crier—when people cry I go right there with them. As soon as Debbie started, my eyes welled up with tears and the pen in my mouth dropped to the floor. I put my arm around Debbie to try to comfort her.

For ten years, Debbie had put her soul into her business, giving it everything she had, sacrificing her personal life in order to give her business life, and yet she didn't have a dime (or a successful business) to show for it. Of course she knew the truth of her struggles all along, but she had chosen to dance around that truth and continue to live in denial.

Putting your nose to the grindstone is a really easy way to cover up for an unhealthy business. We think, if we can just work harder, longer, better—if we can just *hold out*—something good will happen, one day. Something big is just around the corner, right? Something that can wipe away all of the debt, financial stress and worry, just like magic. After all, don't we deserve that? Isn't that how the story is supposed to end?

No, my friend, that's the movies —nothing like what we experience in real life.

When Debbie ran the Instant Assessment, she had to face reality: Her business was on the verge of death and it was taking her down with it. She kept saying, "I am a fool; I am a fool."

Those words tore into me, because I'd been there. I understand exactly how it feels to face the naked truth about my business, my bank account, my strategies and my hard-fought success.

My own wake-up call came in the form of my daughter's piggy bank. My story goes back before that, though, back to when I began to lose my way—the day I received a check for $388,000. It was the first of several checks I would receive for the sale of my second company, a multimillion-dollar computer forensic investigations business I had co-founded, to a Fortune 500 firm. I had now built and sold two companies, and that check was all the proof I needed that my friends and family were right about me: When it came to growing businesses, I had the Midas touch.

The day I received the check, I bought three cars: a Dodge Viper (my college fantasy dream car, something I promised I would get for myself "one day" when I "made it," aka, the "that-guy-must-have-a-tiny-penis-car"), a Land Rover for my wife, and a spare—a tricked-out BMW.

I had always believed in frugality, but now I was rich (with an ego to match). I joined the private club; the one where, the more money you give, the higher they place your name on the members' wall. And I rented a house on a remote Hawaiian island so my wife, my children and I could spend the next three or so weeks experiencing what our new lifestyle would be like. You know, "how the other half lives."

I thought it was time to revel in the money I had created. What I didn't know was, I was about to learn the difference between making money (income) and accumulating money (wealth). These are two very, *very* different things.

I launched my first business on ambition and air, sleeping in my car or under conference room tables when visiting clients in order to avoid the cost of hotels. So imagine the surprised look from my wife, Krista, when I asked the sales guy at the dealership for "the most expensive Land Rover you have." Not the best Land Rover. Not the safest Land Rover. The *most expensive* Land Rover. He skipped his way to the manager, doing a giddy hand-clap.

Krista looked at me and said, "Have you lost your mind? Can we really afford this?"

Full of snark, I said, "Can we afford it? We have more money than God." I will never forget the stupidity coming out of my mouth that day; such disgusting words, such a disgusting ego. Krista was right. I had lost my mind—and, at least for the moment, my soul.

Yup. That day was the beginning of the end. What I was well on my way to discovering was, while I knew how to *make* millions, what I was really, really proficient at doing was *losing* millions.

It wasn't just the lifestyle I bought into that caused my financial downfall. The trappings of success were a symptom of my arrogance—I believed in my own mythology. I was King Midas, reinvented. I could do no wrong. And because I had the golden touch and knew how to build successful businesses, I decided that investing in a dozen brand-new start-ups was the best way to use my windfall. After all, it was only a matter of time before my entrepreneurial genius rubbed off on these promising companies.

Did I care if the founders of these companies knew what they were doing? No—I had all the answers (read that with massive douchey emphasis). I assumed that my golden touch would more than compensate for their lack of business expertise. I hired a team to manage the infrastructure of all of these start-ups—accounting, marketing, social media, web design. I was sure I had the formula for success: a promising start-up, the infrastructure and my incredible, superior, magic touch (more douchey emphasis).

Then, I started writing checks—five thousand to one person, ten thousand to another, every month more checks, and still more. One time, I cut a check for fifty thousand dollars to cover expenses for one of these companies. In retrospect, it was clear that I would not be able to grow all of these companies to the point where they would eventually become niche authorities, as I had with my two previous companies. There was never enough revenue to cover the ever-increasing mountain of bills.

Because of my massive ego, I didn't allow the good people who started these businesses to *become* true entrepreneurs. They were just my pawns. I ignored the signs and kept funneling money into my investments, sure that King Midas would be able to turn it all around.

Within twelve months, all of the companies I invested in, save for one, went belly-up. When I started writing checks to pay bills for companies that had already folded, I realized that I was not an angel investor; I was the Angel of Death.

It was a monumental disaster. Scratch that; *I* was a monumental disaster. Within a couple of years, I lost nearly every penny of my hard-earned fortune. Over half a million in savings gone. A much larger (embarrassingly larger) amount of investment money gone. Worse, I had no incoming revenue. By February 14th of 2008, I was down to my last ten thousand dollars.

I will never forget that Valentine's Day. Not because it was so full of love (even though it was), but because it was the day I realized that the old adage, "When you hit rock bottom, the only way to go is up," is total bullshit. I discovered that day that, when you hit rock bottom, sometimes you get *dragged* along the bottom, scraping your face on every one of those rocks until you're battered, bruised and bloodied.

That morning, I got a call at my office from Keith, my accountant. He said, "Good news, Mike. I got a jump-start on your taxes this year and just finished your return for 2007. You only owe $28,000."

I felt a sharp pain in my chest, like a knife stabbing me. I remember thinking, "Is this what it feels like to have a heart attack?"

I would have to scramble to get the $18,000 I didn't have, and then figure out how to cover my mortgage next month plus all of the small recurring and unexpected expenses that added up to a whole lot of cash.

As Keith wrapped up the call, he said that the bill for his services would arrive on Monday.

"How much?" I asked.

"Two thousand."

I felt the knife twist. I had $10,000 to my name and bills totaling three times that amount. After I ended the call, I put my head on my desk and cried. I had gone so far astray from my values, from who I was at my core, that I had destroyed everything. Now, not only could I not pay my taxes; I had no idea how I would provide for my family.

At the Michalowicz household, Valentine's Day is a legit holiday—on a level with Thanksgiving. We have a special dinner together, exchange cards and go around the table sharing stories about what we love about each other. This is why Valentine's Day is my favorite day of the year. Typically, I would come home with flowers, or balloons, or both. That Valentine's Day I came home with nothing.

Though I tried to hide it, my family knew something was wrong. At the dinner table, Krista asked me if I was okay. That was all it took for the dam to break. The shame was too great. I went from offering up forced smiles to sobbing in a matter of seconds. My children stared at me, shocked and horrified. When I finally stopped crying enough to speak, I said, "I lost everything. Every single penny."

Total. Silence. I slumped over in my chair; the shame was too great for me to face my family, not when all the money I had earned to support them was gone. Not only had I failed to provide for my family; my ego had stolen it all away. To this day I can find no other words to describe it: I felt pure, unadulterated shame about what I had done.

My daughter, Adayla, who was nine years old at the time, got up from the table and ran to her bedroom. I couldn't really blame her—I wanted to run away, too.

The silence continued for two painfully awkward minutes until Adayla walked back into the room carrying her piggy bank, the one she had received as a gift when she was born. It had clearly been cared for; even with all those years of use, there wasn't a single chip or crack on the bank. She had secured the rubber stopper in place with a combination of masking tape, duct tape and rubber bands.

Adayla set her piggy bank down on the dining room table and slid it toward me. Then she said the words that will stay with me until the day I die:

"Daddy, we're going to make it."

That Valentine's Day I woke up feeling like Debbie Horovitch felt after her Instant Assessment: like a fool. But by the end of the day I learned what net worth really is, thanks to my nine-year-old daughter. That day I also learned that no amount of talent, or ingenuity, or passion or skill would change the fact that cash is *still* king. I learned that a nine-year-old girl had mastered the essence of financial security: save your money and block access to it so it doesn't get stolen—by *you*. And I learned that I could tell myself that my natural aptitude for business, my relentless drive and my solid work ethic could overcome any cash crisis, but it would be a lie.

Running the Instant Assessment can be like having a bucket of ice water dropped on your head. Or it can seem like the most humbling moment of your life, like when your daughter volunteers her life savings to save you from the mess you made. But no matter how sharp the pain is, it's better to face it than continue to live and operate your business in denial.

At creativeLIVE, after Debbie calmed down a bit, I said, "The last ten years were not wasted. I understand you feel that way right now, but it's not true. You needed to experience those years to get you where you are today, here with me, doing this. You needed to reach a point where enough is enough." To finally change, she needed her piggy bank moment. We all do.

The truth is, Debbie is far from a fool. Fools never seek out answers. Fools never realize there is a different way, even if it's staring them right in the face. Fools don't admit they need to change. Debbie faced the music, realized what she was doing wasn't working and decided she would not stand for it anymore. Debbie is smart and courageous, and a hero, too. She implored me to put her story in this book and not cloak her name… for you. Debbie wanted you to know you're not alone.

The majority of small businesses, and medium businesses, and even some big ones are barely surviving. That guy driving the new Tesla, whose children go to private school via chauffeur and who lives in a massive house and runs a three million-dollar company, is one bad month from declaring bankruptcy. I should know; he's my neighbor.

The entrepreneur who says "business is great" at the networking event is the same woman who later tries to ask me a question in the parking lot that is indecipherable through her tears; she's crying because she hasn't been able to pay herself a salary for almost a year and will soon be evicted from her home. That particular incident happened last night, twelve hours before I wrote it down to become a story for this book. It's just one of many similar conversations I've had with entrepreneurs who are afraid to tell the truth about their financials.

The Young Entrepreneur of the Year Award recipient who is changing the world, who is lauded as the next generation of genius, who is destined to be on the cover of *Fortune* Magazine because of his business acumen, is taking out bank loan after bank loan and racking up credit card debt to cover payroll behind the scenes. I should know; that was me.

There is no elephant in the room. This dirty little secret is bigger than an elephant—it's King Kong, people! King Kong is in the room. And today is the day we call it what is. Today is the day we draw a line in the sand and never accept it again. Today is the day we make your business (and your life, in the process) financially strong. Permanently.

I have done it for myself. I have done it with companies I partnered with. And I have taught countless others how to do this and watched gleefully as their businesses turned the corner toward profitability.

I promise you, with everything I am, if you follow the system I detail in these pages, this book will do the same for you. The process is simple. Shockingly simple, once you know the trick. Sticking to it is the hard part. So I am going to give you both—how to do it *and* how to stick with it.

You have probably put a lot of work into growing your business. You are probably good or great at that part. That's awesome. And that's surely half of the equation. But colossal growth without financial health will still kill your company. A hot body is useless if its blood is poisoned; money is the lifeblood of your business. With this book, you have an opportunity to master money.

Money is the foundation. Without enough money, we cannot take our message, our products or our services to the world. Without enough money, we are slaves to the businesses we launched. I find this hilarious because, in large part, we started our businesses because we wanted to be free.

Without enough money, we cannot fully realize our authentic selves. Money amplifies who we are. There isn't a single ounce of doubt in my mind that you are intended to do something big on this planet.

You wear the cape of what I believe is the greatest of all superheroes: The Entrepreneur. But your superhero powers can only yield as much power as your energy source provides. Money. You need money, superhero.

When I sat down to evaluate where I went wrong I realized that, while my own spending and arrogance definitely played a part, I also lacked knowledge. I had mastered how to grow businesses quickly, yet I never really graduated to understanding profitability. I had learned how to collect money, for sure, but I had never learned how to keep it, how to control it or how to grow it.

I knew how to grow a business from nothing, working with whatever resources I had; but as revenue increased, so did my spending. I discovered that this was the way I ran both my personal life and my business. I took pride in making magic happen with pennies in my pocket, but as soon as I got some real cash, I made sure that I had a very good reason to spend it. It was a check-to-check lifestyle, but sustainable—as long as sales sustained and did not dip.

While my companies grew explosively, I still operated them on a check-to-check basis—and I had no idea that this was a problem. The point was to grow, right? Increase sales and the profit will take care of itself, right?

Wrong. Money problems occur when one of two things happen:

1. Sales slow down. The problem here is obvious—when we operate check-to-check and sales slow down, we don't have enough to cover expenses.

2. Sales speed up. This problem here is not obvious, but it is insidious. As our income climbs, expenses quickly follow. Consistent incoming cash flow is hard to sustain. Big deposits feel great, but are irregular. Drought periods come quickly and unexpectedly, causing a major gap in cash flow. And cutting back on expenses is nearly impossible because our business (and personal) lifestyle is locked in at our new level. Exchanging the newly leased car for a rust-bucket,

laying off employees because we're overstaffed, saying no to our partners—all of this is very hard to do because of the agreements and promises we made. Cutting expenses becomes impossible because we don't want to admit we've been wrong in how we've been growing our businesses. So rather than reduce our costs in any meaningful way, we scramble to cover ridiculously high expenses. We steal from Peter to pay Paul, hoping for another big payout.

Sound familiar? I thought it might. Over the last five years I've connected with entrepreneurs at every level of growth, and this "top line" (revenue-focused), check-to-check methodology is more common than you may realize. We assume that multimillion-dollar companies are turning big profits, but it's rare to find a truly profitable business. Most entrepreneurs are just covering their monthly nut (or worse) and accumulating massive debt.

We think bigger is better, but so often all we get with a bigger business are *bigger problems.*

Without an understanding of profitability, every business, no matter how big, no matter how "successful," is a house of cards. I made a lot of money with my first two businesses, but not because I ran a tight fiscal ship. I was just lucky enough to keep the plates spinning fast enough and the company growing big enough that someone else was willing to buy it and fix the financial problems.

I sold my first two businesses for a big payout and so did not learn the ultimate financial lesson until after I invested in a dozen more businesses and the lesson came in hard. After my house of cards fell, I set out on a mission to find a better way, a simpler way, a highly effective way to ensure that all businesses, regardless of size and regardless of their current state of affairs, could end the check-to-check cycle and become instantly profitable—without chasing the big payout.

And I found it.

Simply put, the Profit First system flips the accounting formula. To date, entrepreneurs, CEOS, freelancers, everyone in nearly every type of business has been using the "sell, pay expenses, and see what's left over" method of profit creation. This ingrained belief has us sell first, then pay expenses, and let the profit take care of itself. Which it rarely does, because the profit is what's *left over*. An afterthought. Profit surely isn't baked into the daily operations. For many entrepreneurs profit is only considered after the fact. Sometimes monthly. Sometimes quarterly. And way too often, annually, when their accountant is preparing the tax returns.

The old, been-around-forever, profitless formula is:

Sales – Expenses = Profit

The new, Profit First Formula is:

Sales – Profit = Expenses

The math in both formulas is the same. Logically, nothing has changed. But Profit First speaks to human behavior—it accounts for the regular Joes of the world, like me, who have a tendency to spend all of whatever is available to us. So in this regard, with the Profit First flip, *everything* has changed. Now you secure your profit *first,* and run your business on the remaining cash you have left.

It comes down to this—do you want to treat your profitability like leftovers, knowing you may only find scraps or an empty plate? Or do you want to get your full, healthy share right up front? I don't know about you, but I want to get my due portion first.

I have taught the Profit First system to small companies and big companies, to private companies and even public companies. It works for all of them. And it will work for you.

My commitment to you is that, if you follow the Profit First system, your business will become permanently profitable from the moment of your next deposit.

Since I began following the system, I have built two more businesses for myself that are now growing at a healthy rate, profitable right from the start. And the one business that managed to survive my Angel-of-Death spending spree? We implemented Profit First and that business is now not only the leader of its niche; it also turns a profit every month.

In the pages of this book, you will discover how to make your business permanently profitable. The Profit First system is simple—as I said, shockingly so. But don't confuse simple with easy. Understanding what I am about to reveal to you will be a no-brainer. Having the discipline to do it and follow through will be the challenge. I will ready you for both.

Provided you take each action step I recommend, you will have transformed your business by the end of Chapter 5. Do I want you to read the rest of the book? Hell yes! In fact, if you want to fully realize your potential as a business leader and take your business where you *know* it was meant to go, you need to read the rest of the book. Consider Chapters 6 through 12 the intermediate and advanced courses in Profit First, in which you will learn all of the methods, tactics and tweaks that will ensure your cash cow continues to make your life easier, happier and more fulfilling. In essence, Chapters 1 through 5 will revive your business. Chapters 6 through 12 will revive *you*.

Following the Profit First system will take courage and dedication; it will require you to set your own ego aside. The payoff is worth it, so worth it.

If you will commit to fixing your business's financials once and for all, you'll never have to pull off a last-minute miracle to cover *anything* again. You'll never have to have your own "piggy bank" moment, as I did, or feel like a fool, as my friend Debbie did when she first realized the financial reality of her business.

When you commit to following the simple but powerful Profit First system, you will finally reap the rewards of entrepreneurship, cashing in on your business—while *still running it*—over and over again, like clockwork.

Today is the day you say enough is enough. Whether your business is experiencing occasional financial stress or total financial horror, today is the day we fix it. Today is the day your business becomes permanently profitable.

# 1 TAMING THE BEAST

I AM Dr. Frankenstein.

Okay, not *the* Dr. Frankenstein, but I am definitely part of the family. I'm probably his long lost twin brother, or something. Or maybe an estranged heir to his (mis)fortune. Maybe you are, too.

If you read Mary Shelley's classic, *Frankenstein,* you know exactly what I'm talking about. The good doctor reanimated life. From mismatched body parts, he stitched together a living being more monster than man. Of course, his creation wasn't a monster at first. No, at first it was a miracle. Dr. Frankenstein brought to life something that, without his extraordinary idea and exhaustive hard work, would not exist.

That's what I did. That's what you did. We brought something to life that didn't exist before we dreamed it up; we created a business out of thin air. Impressive! Miraculous! Beautiful! Or at least it was, until the monster revealed itself.

Stitching together a business with nothing but a great idea, your unique talents and whatever few resources you have at hand is most certainly a miracle. And it feels like one, too. Until the day you realize your business has become a giant, scary, soul-sucking, cash-eating monster. That's the day you discover that you, too, are an esteemed member of the Frankenstein family.

And, just as happened in Shelley's book, mental and physical torment ensues. You try to tame the monster, but you can't. The monster wreaks destruction at every turn: empty bank accounts, credit card debt, loans and an ever-increasing list of "must-pay" expenses. He eats up your time, too. You wake up before sunrise to work, and you're still at it long after the sun goes down. You work and work, yet the monster continues to loom. Your relentless work doesn't free you; it further drains you. Trying to keep the monster at bay before it destroys your entire world is exhausting. You suffer sleepless nights, worries about collection calls—sometimes from your own employees—and a near-constant panic about how to cover next week's bills with a few dollars and the lint in your pocket.

What is the only way out we can see? Growth. It is the battle cry of nearly every entrepreneur and business leader. Grow! Grow! Grow! Bigger sales. Bigger customers. Bigger investors.

The only problem is, it doesn't work.

Growth is only half the equation. It is a critical half, but still only half. Have you ever seen the guys at the gym with the massive arms and heaving chests, the ones as big as oxen who also have toothpick legs? They're only working half the equation and have become unhealthy freaks as a result. Sure, that guy can throw a monster punch, but God forbid he needs to step into it, or move a little. His puny legs will give out instantly; he'll curl up on the floor and cry like a baby.

Most business owners try to grow their way out of their problems, hinging salvation on the next big sale or customer or investor, but the result is simply a bigger monster. (And the bigger your company gets, the more anxiety you deal with. If both are cash-eating monsters, a $300,000 company is much easier to manage than a $3,000,000 company. I know; I have survived operating both, and bigger.) This is constant growth without concern for health. And the day that big sale or customer or investor doesn't show, *you* will fall to the ground and curl up crying like a baby.

If you think operating your business is closer to a horror story than to a fairy tale, you're not alone. Since I wrote my first book, *The Toilet Paper Entrepreneur,* I've met thousands of entrepreneurs; and let me tell you, most are struggling to tame the beast that is their business. Many companies—even those that appear to have it all together, even the big guys who seem to dominate their industries—struggle to stay afloat.

I'll never forget meeting the owner of a $15,000,000 company who furnished his house with plastic lawn furniture because he couldn't afford the real stuff. What does it say when the leader of a multimillion-dollar company can't even swing a trip to Ikea? It would make anyone question his true wealth, and the wealth and health of his business.

So what's the solution? How do you not only make it out of this situation alive, but also build the miracle of a business you originally envisioned, a business that serves you, a business that provides *for* you? The solution isn't a bigger monster. The solution surely isn't a second and third monster. The solution isn't killing your existing monster, or even hacking it apart and stitching it back together into a tiny monster. In fact, the solution is shockingly simple and surprisingly effective.

It begins by working with your natural tendencies, not against them.

CHECK-TO-CHECK AND PANIC-TO-PANIC

Have you ever had the thought that the universe knows exactly how much extra money you have? A customer pays up on a $4000 past-due invoice you wrote off months ago and later that week your delivery truck breaks down—for good. Bye-bye, $4000. You land a new client and a wad of cash drops into your lap; only minutes later you remember that this is a three-payroll month. Oh well, at least now you'll almost be able to cover it. Or you get a credit on your credit card account for an accidental billing (woo hoo, found money!), only to discover another charge on your credit card for something that you forgot all about.

It's not the universe that knows how much we have in our bank accounts. It's us. We default to managing the cash of our business by doing what I call "bank balance accounting."

If you're like most entrepreneurs, and me, this is how it works:

You look at your bank balance and see a chunk of change. Yippee! You feel great for about ten minutes, and then decide to pay all the bills that have been piling up. The balance goes to zero and very quickly you feel that all-too-familiar tightening in the chest as your throat dries up (or any number of symptoms of stress).

What do we do when, instead of a decent bank balance, we see that there's next to nothing there? We immediately panic a little (or a lot). We hit "go" mode: need to sell fast! Need to make collection calls! Need to pretend the bills never arrived, or send out checks and "accidentally" forget to sign them. When we know our bank balance is super low (I'm talking limbo "how low can you go"-low), we'll do anything to buy the only thing we can afford: time.

I'm going to go out on a limb and guess that you only look at your income statement on occasion. I suspect you rarely look at your cash flow statements or balance sheet. And if you do, I doubt you review these docs on a daily basis or understand exactly what they say. Bet you check your bank account every day, though? It's okay. If you look at your bank account daily, I want to congratulate you, because that means you are a typical—scratch that—a *normal* business leader; that's how most entrepreneurs behave.

It's human nature to look at what you have *right now* and make decisions based on that information. This is called the "Recency Effect," the psychological phenomenon in which we humans (that's you, by the way) place a disproportionate significance on what we experienced most recently. For example, if I ask you to recall the last few words I wrote, you will easily recall this sentence (the most recent), but good luck remembering two sentences ago.

Recent stuff is the big stuff; all the other stuff becomes a waning memory. How does the Recency Effect apply to your finances? If you deposit lots of money today, you will probably feel great, the outlook for your business will appear to be good and all will seem well. That's the Recency Effect. If, on the other hand, your bank account is bone dry, you might feel hopeless and your business may seem like a horrible mess. (Maybe as though it's a monster?) That's the Recency Effect. It is a trap because it dictates our behavior.

Also in our nature as entrepreneurs is the desire to find problems and fix them. This is how we manage money. When we have enough money in the bank, we think we don't have money problems, and so we focus on other challenges. When we see that we don't have enough money in the bank, we go on red alert and take immediate action to fix our money problems, usually by trying to collect revenue quickly, or sell a big-ticket item or some combination of the two.

We use the money we have to pay the bills we owe; when we don't have enough to cover everything, we try to get more money through sales and collections. Except that to support new revenue, we now have a host of new related expenses, so the cycle starts all over again. If you haven't relied on it from the start, eventually the only "solution" is to take on debt—a second mortgage on your family home, a line of credit tied to your building, a stack of credit cards three inches high. This is how many entrepreneurs end up operating their businesses check-to-check and panic-to-panic.

So let me ask you a question. How easy would it be to grow your business if you operated this way? Do you think you'd ever be able to get off this roller coaster ride? Could you dig yourself out of debt using this system? Of course not.

And yet bank balance accounting is human nature. We humans are not big on change. Change is hard. With your very best intentions, changing your natural tendencies to operate your business based on how much cash you see in your account would take years. I don't know, you tell me—do you have years to make your own transformation before your very own monster destroys everything? I sure as hell didn't.

This is why, if we are to free ourselves from living check-to-check and panic-to-panic, we must find a method that works *with* our nature, not against it.

Without an effective money management system that does not require massive mindset change, we get stuck in trying to sell our way out of our struggles. Sell more. Sell faster. Get money any way you can. It is trap—a dangerous trap that would even have Frankenstein's monster poopin' his panties. It's the Survival Trap.

THE SURVIVAL TRAP

This is how the Survival Trap works. Take a look at Figure 1 on the next page. We are at point A (which is really called crisis) and we want to get to point B (which is our vision for our future). The thing is, our vision is usually very vague. Instead of a clear statement of our products or services and the clients we want to serve, it might be

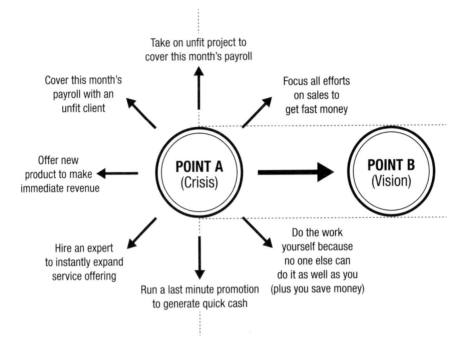

Figure 1: The Survival Trap

something like, "I want a lot of money and some relief from stress." The connection between Point A and Point B is never defined, beyond, "Sell, baby! Just sell!" And "just selling" is a huge part of the trap, for three reasons:

First, any sale feels like a good sale, because sales help to temporarily lift you out of crisis. Now look at the figure. You can see that many of the decisions we make around "just selling" in fact take us *farther away* from our vision.

Maybe you start offering a new service, or add a new product, because it will make fast money, but never even consider that it has nothing to do with what you want your company to become or whom you want your company to serve.

Take for example my lawn guy, Ernie. He, like most lawn guys in the Northeast, makes tons of money removing leaves. This past fall he knocked on my door and said that he noticed leaves in my gutters and would gladly clean them up. He has a captive client (me), and can now sell me another service. Easy money. When he was on the roof, he noticed my shingles needed repair. He offered roofing services. Why not repair my chimney, too?

It is very easy to go from being a guy who rakes lawns to a guy who fixes chimneys because of the opportunity for "easy money" with captive clients. The money may be easy, but what about the costs to do it all? Rakes and blowers for yard work are useless when working on roofs or chimneys. Now this guy needs ladders, roofing gear, bricks and other materials. And most importantly, he needs the skills to complete the tasks, which means hiring skilled labor or going back to raking, gutter-cleaning, roofing and chimney school. Each new "easy sale" took Ernie farther from his vision for his lawn-raking business.

The Survival Trap promises fast wealth, but when we're caught in it we rarely think about the massive cost of opportunity; and most of the time, we can't discern profitable income from debt-generating income. Instead of being the world's best at one thing, mastering the process of delivering perfectly and super-efficiently, we end up doing a greater variety of things and become less and less efficient at each step, while our businesses become more and more costly to run.

The Survival Trap is not about driving toward our vision. It is all about taking action, any action, to get out of crisis. Any of the actions shown in Figure 1 will get a us out of an immediate crisis. But, by taking actions like those on the left of the circle, we get out of crisis, sure enough, but we are going in the opposite direction from our vision at Point B. Other actions shown on the diagram don't take us in the opposite direction, but are askew. Only when you stay in the channel of the horizontal dotted lines do you make your vision for your business a reality.

All of the "just sell" actions we take in the moment bring temporary relief. They get us out of immediate crisis, but when the money dries up again the following day, and as the expenses grow the following week or month, we find ourselves in crisis again and the pattern repeats. We take money from anyone (and I mean anyone) willing to pay us. Money from bad clients. Money for bad projects. Money from our own pockets (if there's anything left in them besides two dimes, a stick of gum and a wad of lint). In this way, we stay stuck on the roller coaster ride that is surviving check-to-check and panic-to-panic.

Second, the Survival Trap is deceptive because it fools us into *thinking* we are at least inching toward our vision. Consider the actions on the right side of the Figure 1. For instance, a "just sell" approach will, by pure happenstance, also occasionally move us toward our vision, we can easily trick ourselves into believing that we're on the right track. Sometimes we make a crisis decision without considering our vision or the path to get there and we get it right. Happenstance happens. At that point we say, "See! I'm getting there. Things are clicking. Things are coming together." But this is random chance, resulting from crisis, not focus or clarity, and therefore false. It is like believing that because you once won on a scratch-off card, the lottery is a good investment strategy. And it is this kind of thinking that quickly lands us back in crisis mode.

Last, when we're stuck in the Survival Trap, we focus our attention on revenue generation first and foremost. Any client (who pays) is a good client. Any work (that makes money) is good work. Crisis makes us panic about money. We need more money now! Never forget: All revenue is *not* the same. Some revenue costs you significantly more in time and money; some costs you less. You must distinguish between the two, since one is profitable and the other puts you out of business.

I explained the Profit First system to my friend Debra Courtright many years back. Debra runs DAC Management, a bookkeeping business. (I'll give you one guess at her middle initial.) Since the day she integrated the Profit First system, Debra has saved company after company using these principles, the exact principles I am about to teach you. Actually, she has more than just saved companies; she consistently turns business after business into cash cows.

Over the years, we have discussed the effects of Profit First on her clients and made some tweaks along the way. She has shared many stories, always removing the names of the guilty. When Debra told me the story I am about to share with you, my jaw dropped. The story is about someone I've never met, about a business I've never visited, but it's a perfect example of the Survival Trap, played out.

Debra received an inquiry from Alex, a prospective client. When she called Debra, Alex was literally gasping for air on the other end of the line. The owner of a local bistro, Alex did not have enough money in the bank to pay her employees or vendors, let alone herself. Her accounting was so messed up she didn't even know to whom she owed money.

Debra immediately implemented a customized version of Profit First (something I will teach you to do for yourself in Chapter 4). While setting up a Profit Account, Owner's Pay Account, Tax Account and Operating Expenses Account, she asked Alex where she kept the sales tax records.

Alex looked at her blankly and said, "What do you mean?"

Turns out, Alex had been charging customers seven percent sales tax, but rather than reporting the earnings and sending the tax to the government, she was using the money to pay other bills.

Debra explained the consequences. "If you don't pay the taxes you collect, you are breaking the law. The state's tax authority can come in here unannounced, shut everything down and walk away with every asset you have. Then they will send you to jail, broke and in debt."

Alex thought she had time to sort everything out, but the very next week, Debra's warning became a reality. The tax reps from the state showed up unannounced at Alex's bistro.

They decided to show her mercy. In front of her customers and employees, they emptied the cash register and handed Alex a letter that basically said, "Pay your sales taxes immediately, or we will shut you down and send you to jail." Cue the next anxiety attack, and Alex's next breathless call to Debra. And yes, that is the tax man showing mercy.

The Survival Trap is an ugly beast. It buys you time, but the monster gets bigger and bigger. And at some point it will destroy you.

Sustained profitability depends on efficiency. You can't become efficient in crisis. In crisis, we justify making money at any cost, right now, even if it means skipping taxes or selling our souls. In crises, the Survival Trap becomes our modus operandi—until our survival strategies create a new, more devastating crisis that scares us straight, as it did Alex, or, more commonly, scares us right out of business.

Part of the problem is bank balance accounting—looking at the money in your bank account as one pool from which you can operate your business without first addressing tax issues or your own salary, never mind profit. This leads to top line thinking—focusing on revenue first, last, and always. That thinking is supported by the traditional accounting method public companies must use and most small businesses elect to use: GAAP (Generally Accepted Accounting Principles).

GAAP IS KILLING YOUR BUSINESS

Since the dawn of time—or shortly thereafter—businesses have kept track of their earnings and expenditures using essentially the same method:

Sales – Expenses = Profit

If you manage the numbers like most entrepreneurs, you start with sales (the top line) and then subtract costs directly related to the delivery of your offering (product or service). Then you subtract all the other costs you incur to run your business: rent, utilities, office supplies and other administrative expenses, sales commissions, taking your client out to lunch, signage, insurance, etc., etc. Then you pay taxes. Then, and only then, do you take your owner's distribution (owner's salary, profit distribution, etc.).

Let's be honest, entrepreneurs hardly ever take anything close to a real salary, and good luck telling the government that you decided to skip taxes this year so that you could pay yourself. Finally, after all that, you post your company's profit. And if your experience is like the majority of entrepreneurs, you never get to "finally." When you're waiting for the leftovers, at best you'll get scraps.

This method ultimately became formalized in the early 1900s. The particulars are updated regularly, but the core system remains the same. Start with sales. Subtract direct costs (the costs you directly incur to create and deliver your product or service). Pay employees. Subtract indirect costs. Pay taxes. Pay owners (owner distributions). Retain or distribute profit (the bottom line). Even if you outsource your bookkeeping or keep a shoebox of receipts under your bed, you know the basic idea.

Logically, GAAP makes complete sense. It suggests that we sell as much as we can, spend as little as we can and pocket the difference. But humans aren't logical. (One episode of *Bridezilla* pretty much proves that.) Just because GAAP makes logical sense doesn't mean it makes "human sense." GAAP both supersedes our natural behavior and makes us believe bigger is better. So we try to sell more. We try, and try, and try to sell our way to success. We do everything we can to make the top line (revenue) grow so that something, anything, will drip down to the bottom line. It becomes a relentless cycle of chasing after every shiny object disguised as opportunity (that's "little pumpkins" to my peeps—you know who you are).

Throughout this haphazard, often desperate, growth process, our expenses are lost in the wash—we just pay as we go. They're all necessary, right? Or at least we think so. Who knows? We're too busy hunting down sales and trying to deliver on all of our promises to worry about the impact of expenses!

We try to spend less without considering investments versus costs. We don't think about leveraging our spending to get way more mileage out of way less. We can't. The more variety of stuff we sell, the more our cost of doing businesses rises. We need to spend more to grow. They say it takes money to make money. But how come no one ever told us what that really translates to: It takes *more* money to make *less* money.

As our monster gets bigger, the need to feed the beast gets out of hand. Now we're faced with covering expenses for more employees, more stuff, more everything. The monster grows. And grows. And grows. Meanwhile, we're still dealing with the same problems, just bigger: more empty bank accounts, higher stacks of credit card bills, bigger loans and an ever-increasing list of "must-pay" expenses. Sound familiar, Dr. Frankenstein?

GAAP's fundamental flaw is, it goes against human nature. No matter how much income we generate, we will always find a way to spend it—all of it. And we have good reasons for all of our spending choices. Everything is justified. Everything is necessary. Soon enough, whatever money we had in the bank dwindles down to nothing as we struggle to cover every "necessary" expense. We get caught in the trap of sell-grow-spend, sell-grow-spend.

How do you think Debra's client Alex ended up in her predicament? Do you think she said, "It's a beautiful day today—I think I'll steal from the government"? Heck, no. She had convinced herself that she needed the sales tax income she collected *right now,* and when "later" came, she wasn't prepared to cover it.

A secondary flaw is this: GAAP teaches us to focus on sales and expenses first. Once again, it works against our human nature, which urges us to grow what we focus on. Remember the lesson of the Recency Effect; it plays out again with the focus on sales and expenses. There is a saying: "What gets measured, gets done." GAAP has us measure sales first (it is the top line, after all), and therefore we sell like mad while expenses are treated like a necessary evil to support— you guessed it—more sales. We spend all that we have, because we believe we must. And we use terms like "plowback" or "reinvest" to feel good about it. Profit? Your salary? Mere afterthoughts. *Leftovers.*

Another problem with GAAP is, it is overwhelmingly complex. You need to hire an accountant to get it right, and when you ask the accountant the details about GAAP, he is likely to get confused. The system changes and is up for interpretation. And we can play games with GAAP: Move some numbers around and post stuff in different spots and the numbers look different. Just ask Enron—they were able to post profits as they were going bankrupt. Yuck!

At the end of the day, the start of a new day, and every second in between, cash is all that counts. It is the lifeblood of your business. Do you have it or not? If you don't, you're in trouble, and if you do, you can sustain.

GAAP was never intended to only manage cash. It is a system for understanding all the elements of your business. It has three key reports: the income statement, the cash flow statement and the balance sheet. There is no question that you need to understand these reports, since they will give you a holistic view of your company; they are powerful and highly useful tools. But the essence of GAAP (Sales - Expenses = Profit) is horribly flawed. It is a formula that builds monsters. It is the Frankenstein Formula.

To successfully run a profitable business, we need a super-simple system to manage our cash, one we can understand without help from an accountant, one that is designed for humans, not Spock.

We need a system that can instantly tell us the truth about the health of our businesses, one that we can look at and know instantly what we need to do to get healthy; a system that tells us what we can actually spend and what needs to be reserved; a system that doesn't require us to change, but automatically works with our natural behaviors.

Profit First is that system.

• • •

The ending of *Frankenstein* is not happy or nicey-nice. The monster destroys everything in Dr. Frankenstein's life—his wife, his family, his hope for the future—so he sets out to exact revenge and kill his creation. The hunt for the monster takes a toll on Dr. Frankenstein and he dies a wrecked man, the monster close behind him. *Frankenstein* is a scary parallel to the extremes of entrepreneurship. Monster businesses have killed marriages, torn apart families and, for some entrepreneurs, decimated any hope for the good life. That miracle of a business we created can end up causing untold suffering; when that happens, the hatred Dr. Frankenstein had for his monster is all too often the chief emotion entrepreneurs have toward their businesses.

But your story doesn't have to end that way. You can have your happily ever after. The good news is that, while your business may seem to be a monster controlling your life, it is also powerful. Whether your annual revenue is $50,000, $500,000, $5,000,000 or even $50,000,000, your business can become a profit-generating workhorse.

Never forget the power of your "monster"—you just have to understand how to direct and control it. When you learn this simple system, your business will no longer be a monster; it will become an obedient, pasture-loving cash cow. A damn strong one, at that.

It worked for Alex, the coffee-shop owner who neglected to pay her sales tax and paid the consequences. Working with Debra, her accountant, and applying Profit First, Alex has paid off all of her taxes and penalties. It took three years to recover, but now Alex is current with her taxes and is running a profitable business. She has fewer employees, but they are fantastic and run the place like clockwork. Business is humming, and freshly ground coffee is always brewing.

What I am about to share with you is going to make your business profitable immediately and determinately. I don't care what size business you have or how long you have been surviving check-to-check and panic-to-panic, month after month and year after year. You are about to be profitable. Forevermore. No more leftovers for you—it's time for you to eat first.

Here's the deal. There is only one way to fix your financials: by facing your financials. You can't ignore them. You can't let someone else take care of them. You need to take charge of the numbers. But there is good news—the process is really, really easy. In fact, you will fundamentally understand it, and implement it, within just a few more chapters.

ACTION STEPS
GET YOUR HEAD IN THE GAME

Step 1: Draw the line in the sand. Agree that, as of today, you are turning over a new leaf. Commit to yourself, and to me, that you will run a profitable business and make everything else secondary to that goal. Email me (my contact info is on my website, and I do read my own email) and decree that you are drawing a line in the sand. Today is the day your business becomes healthy. Permanently. Don't wait another second.

Step 2: Agree not to beat yourself up. I don't care what your business financials look like today. I don't care if your business is on the verge of going under, or if you just want to ramp up your profits even higher. Every business can be improved with Profit First. The only thing that will get in our way is if you bitch, moan and cry about the past. So that will not be permitted. I am granting you a clean slate. And you are promising me that you aren't going to complain about the past. Together, we are just going to get to work and fix it.

# 2 HOW PROFIT FIRST WORKS

I T's funny how losing nearly all of your money can cause you to watch a lot of late-night network TV. What? Before you side-eye me, this was right after I lost all of my money to my own arrogance, so cable TV was the first thing to go. Insomnia brought about by anxiety does *not* equal better quality sleep, so that pretty much left me with two options: Stare at the ceiling or watch late-night network TV, courtesy of my twelve-dollar, indoor rabbit-ear antenna (yes, antennae still work and, even with the fancy modern digital signal, the reception still sucks).

Most infomercials pitch instant cures. Eat only grapefruit for ten weeks, and presto! You're thin. Drink this magic goo three times a day and before you know it you'll be able to bounce a quarter off your ripped abs! Wrap this electromagnetic thingamajig around your waist, electrocute yourself every five seconds, and you'll have a teeny-tiny waist in less than six weeks, all while never getting off the couch to clean the Doritos off your shirt!

One late night, I had had enough of the infomercials and turned on PBS to find, sure enough, a fitness guy talking about diets. (Was God trying to tell me something? I stopped working out for a little bit, but. . . jeez!)

The fitness expert explained to the studio audience that the quick fixes lauded by late-night infomercials didn't work (thank you!) and that they weren't sustainable. He said that what we really need are simple *lifestyle* fixes that do not require us to change our natural tendencies, changes that make an impact before we have a chance to screw it up with our unhealthy food choices. And his first fix suggestion? Smaller plates.

Now riveted, I watched as the man explained that our natural human behavior is to fill our plates with food and, because Mom said so, clean that plate right up by eating everything on it. I still don't get Mom's logic—there are children starving in Africa, so I need to get fat? But the "clean-your-plate club" was instilled in me and probably in you, too. The message is ingrained. Changing that habit for a day is a no-brainer. But changing it permanently? That's hard. Some would say it's nearly impossible. This is why so many people who diet gain the weight back, why people rarely follow through on New Year's resolutions past the end of January, and why it's so difficult to be disciplined with your spending.

As I continued to watch the program, the expert went on to say that rather than work to change our "eat everything on the plate" behavior we simply need to change the size of our plates. When we use smaller plates, we dish out smaller portions, thus eating fewer calories while continuing our natural human behavior of serving a full plate and eating all of what is served.

I sat straight up on the couch, my mind alert with this new revelation. The solution is not to try to change our ingrained habits, which is really hard to pull off and nearly impossible to sustain; but instead to change the structure around us and *leverage* those habits.

It was then that I realized: Every penny my company made was going onto one plate, and I was gobbling it all up, using every last scrap to operate my business. Every dollar that came in went into one account, my operating account, and I was "eating it all."

It hurts to admit this, but I was never good at money management. I thought I was, but looking back now, I realize how bad I was at managing money. I thought I was frugal in principle, or because I was a savvy entrepreneur. But in truth, I was frugal in my businesses because it was forced upon me.

When I started my first company, a computer network integrator (today it would be called a managed service provider), I had no money. I was able to sell, service, run my office—I could do all that stuff with practically no money because I didn't have any. As the business grew, I started to spend. The more I made, the more I spent, and I believed that all expenditures were necessary. We needed better equipment, a better office (an unfinished basement is no place for a business). I brought on people to do the work so I could sell more. Every step forward in sales growth required an equal step up in my infrastructure, human resources, grade-A office space or whatever (all fancy terms for expenses).

After losing it all, I discovered that I work with whatever is put in front of me. Give me a hundred dollars and I will make it happen. Give me a hundred grand and I will make it happen. And while a hundred thousand-dollars made it easier to make it happen, it also made it way easier to make mistakes. Totally waste a few hundred dollars when you have a hundred thousand at your disposal, and you feel nothing. Totally waste a few hundred bucks, when you only have a few hundo to your name, and you feel that pain fast and hard.

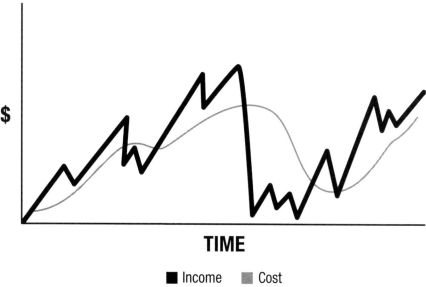

TIME

■ Income   ■ Cost

Figure 2: Income vs. Cost

Looking back at my companies, I realized that I grew them quickly but still survived check-to-check, only making the real money when I sold them. As my incoming cash increased (the darker line on Figure 2), my expenses increased at a similar rate (lighter line). The only time I would have a profit was when income jumped up and I didn't have time to spend at the same rate. However, I would quickly ramp up my expenses to serve my "new level of sales." Then sales would settle back down, or drop, while my new level of expenses remained higher. Losses accumulated. The desperate need to sell more, faster, increased.

I muted the television and began to connect the dots. I wondered, "If I reduce the 'plate size' of my business's operating account, will I spend differently?" Looking back at my past behavior, the answer came quickly. Yes, I would. So rather than try to curb my spending habit, I would create the experience of having less cash on hand than I actually had. How did I know this would work? Because it already works for millions of people, with every paycheck—think 401K deductions.

Excited, I realized that, as with a 401K, if I were truly going to believe that the money I had left over in the bank after reducing my deposits from revenue (my small plate) was all I had to work with, whatever money I took off the top would have to go into a separate account that would not be easy for me to see, let alone access. Investment accounts charge penalties for early withdrawals to dissuade investors from drawing from their accounts, and I needed something similar in place to stop me from borrowing from the separate account.

But what would I *do* with the "other money?" Could I use it to— shock of shocks—*pay myself a salary?* Pay my taxes?

Hey. Hey wait. Wait one stinkin' minute. Could I actually set aside some of it for profit—*before* I paid bills?

And that's when it hit me—what if I took my profit *first?*

For a guy who built two businesses on top line (revenue focused) thinking, this was a revelation. At 3:00 a.m., it sounded like crazy talk. Who would have the audacity to take profit first?

Me.

WHAT THE DIET INDUSTRY KNOWS ABOUT GROWING A HEALTHY BUSINESS

A 2012 report by Koert Van Ittersum and Brian Wansink in the *Journal of Consumer Research* identifies the average plate size in America as having grown 23% between the years 1900 and 2012, from 9.6 inches to 11.8 inches. Running the math, the article explains that, should this increase in plate size encourage an individual to consume just fifty more calories per day, that person would put on an extra five pounds of weight... each year. Year after year, that adds up to a very chunky monkey.

But using smaller plates is just one factor. A Twinkie on a small plate is still a Twinkie.

There is more to a healthy diet, based on four core principles of weight loss and nutrition. These four principles are exactly the same foundation for business health.

1. **Use Small Plates** – Using smaller plates starts a chain reaction. When you use a small plate, you get smaller portions, which means you take in fewer calories. When you take in fewer calories than you normally would, you start to lose weight.

2. **Serve Sequentially** – Eat the vegetables, rich in nutrients and vitamins, first. If you leave them to eat last, you will rarely finish your vegetables. They'll just sit there piled up on the side of the plate.

3. **Remove Temptation** – Remove any temptation from where you eat. People are driven by convenience. If when you're hungry, junk food is easily accessible, you're more likely to eat it. If you don't have any junk food in the house, you're probably not going to run out to the store to get it. (That would mean putting on pants.) You're going to eat the healthy food you stocked, instead. My weakness is Chocodiles: Twinkies covered in dark chocolate and wrapped in love. Fortunately, they stopped making them. But if one sneaked into my house, even if it had expired in 1972, I would devour that delicious elixir of love and monounsaturated fats. Now, I always make sure I have healthy options with me, and the junk is locked away.

4. **Enforce a Rhythm** – Don't eat when you're hungry; it is already too late, and you will binge. Instead, eat frequently so that you never get hungry. You will actually consume fewer calories this way.

Profit First is a simple, "small plate" diet philosophy. In the Introduction I shared the basic formula of Profit First and how it differs from the accounting method most businesses use.

The old profit-as-"leftovers" formula (what I like to call the Frankenstein Formula):

$$Sales - Expenses = Profit$$

The new Profit First Formula:

$$Sales - Profit = Expenses$$

What you are about to learn isn't anything new. It is something I suspect you have been aware of—in full or at least in part—but have never done. It is the concept of "pay yourself first" meets "small plate servings" meets "Grandma's hidden stash of money in the cookie jar" meets your pre-existing natural, human tendencies.

Here's how Profit First is like a successful diet:

1. **Use Small Plates** – When money comes into your main operating account, immediately disperse it into different accounts in predetermined percentages. Each of these accounts has a different objective: one is for profit, one for owner pay, another for taxes and another for operating expenses. These are the four basic accounts and where you should get started, but you will get more advanced in account setup as we move along.

2. **Serve Sequentially** – Always, *always* move money to your Profit Account first, then to your Owner Pay Account and then to your Tax Account, with what remains to expenses. Always in that order. No exceptions. Move it, stash it and let it accumulate. And if there isn't enough money left for expenses? This does *not* mean you need to pull from the other accounts. What it *does* mean is, you can't afford those expenses and need to get rid of them. This will bring more health to your business than you can ever imagine.

3. **Remove Temptation** – Move your Profit Account and other accounts out of arm's reach. Make it really hard and painful to get to that money, thereby removing the temptation to "borrow" (i.e., steal) from yourself. Use an accountability mechanism to prevent access, except for the right reason.

4. **Enforce A Rhythm** – Do your payables twice a month (specifically, on the 10th and 25th). Don't pay only when money is piled up in the account. Get into a rhythm of paying bills twice a month so you can see how cash accumulates and where the money really goes. This is controlled, recurring and frequent cash flow management, not by-the-seat-of-your-pants cash management.

When I started applying this small plate philosophy to my company's finances, I was doing consulting work and speaking on entrepreneurship. I also applied my new Profit First system to my one surviving investment, Hedgehog Leatherworks.

At the time, I was putting the finishing touches on my first business book, *The Toilet Paper Entrepreneur,* into which I inserted a small section about the concept of Profit First Accounting (PFA). After the book came out I continued to refine the system, exploring and living it, and everything changed. I started implementing it with other entrepreneurs. And it worked—for me, for them and for my readers. I started getting calls from people who had read the book and tried basic PFA, creating amazing results. I also decided to drop the "A" from PFA—partly because Profit First is not an accounting system (it simply plugs into your accounting system) and partly because, when I heard Facebook used to be called "The Facebook" and dropped the "The" to sound cooler, I thought I would follow suit and drop a word.

Fueled by my passion for entrepreneurship and my determination to be profitable *now*, not at some indeterminate date in the future, I set about to perfect my system. In that process I discovered other entrepreneurs and business leaders who were running their businesses check-to-check and desperately needed the Profit First system. But I also found entrepreneurs and business leaders who had been implementing a similar system to great success. People like my barber, Lou Leone, the second-generation owner of a barbershop that has been profitable from day one. And Phil Tirone, who, while building his first, highly profitable multimillion-dollar business, continued to rent the same studio apartment until he determined that he had secured enough profit to upgrade—to a one bedroom.

In the coming pages, I will share these stories and more: stories about people who are in lockstep with their profits and stories about other folks, like you and me, who were giving it their all but still ended up only breaking even on their best days—people who now turn a profit every month and enjoy the fruits of their labors. People like Jose and Jorge, two entrepreneurs who started using Profit First from the first day they discovered it and have not only experienced very respectable growth, but have continuously taken in a 7% to 20% percent profit, month after month.

Your story isn't finished yet. Not in the least. It's time to create your happy, kickass chapter.

ACTION STEPS

GET YOUR BUSINESS PROFIT-READY

Step 1: Set up the small plates with your bank. You will need four accounts: Profit Account, Owner's Pay Account, Tax Account and Operating Expenses Account.

You probably already have one or two accounts with your bank (checking and savings). Keep the checking account as your Operating Expenses Account and set up Tax and Profit as savings accounts (these are simply holding bins), with Owner's Pay as another checking account.

Some banks limit the number of transfers in and out of savings accounts. This shouldn't be a problem, since we will be using a rhythm. However, if your Tax or Profit Accounts are checking accounts, that is fine. The goal is not to get a little extra interest; the goal is to hold money temporarily and remove temptation. Some banks charge fees or have minimum balance requirements. Don't let that deter you. Speak to the bank manager and negotiate the fees and requirements. If the manager is unwilling to negotiate, find a new bank.

Step 2: Set up two more external savings accounts with a bank other than the bank you use for daily operations. One account will be your no-temptation Profit Account. The second will be your no-temptation Tax Account. Set them up with the ability to withdraw money directly from the respective savings accounts in your original bank.

Step 3: Don't enable any of the "convenience" options for your two external accounts. You don't need or want to view these accounts online. You don't want checkbooks for these accounts. You just want to deposit your income and forget it… for now.

3 THE NAKED TRUTH

I T'S inevitable. Whenever two or more entrepreneurs are gathered together, one of them will ask the "How big is it?" question. It's always some version of the same—"How big is your business?" It might sound like, "How many employees do you have?" Or, "How many territories do you cover?" Or, if you're one of those straight-to-the-point types (like a few of my classmates at the high school reunion), you might even be so bold as to ask, "How much did you take in last year?" However it's phrased, I hear some version of the "How big is it?" question wherever I go—it's like a law of the entrepreneurial (and porn) community!

Many years ago, I joined a global entrepreneurial organization to learn from successful, more experienced business leaders from all over the country. At one of our meetings, I met my buddy Phil Tirone, founder of 720CreditScore.com. Phil made his first fortune in the mortgage lending industry in California, so he knows a thing or two about *real* wealth. Not the top line, or the outward appearance. The bottom line. The actual take home money. *The naked truth.*

"When you get a loan, you take down your pants. You can't hide anything," Phil told me as we enjoyed iced coffee outside his Phoenix home, staring at Camelback Mountain in the distance.

"There are things that people don't want to talk about. You don't want to talk about your lack of profit. You don't want to talk about putting a second mortgage on your home to help run your business. You surely don't want to admit to being the guy that has five times more credit card debt than the average family in our debtors' nation. After fourteen years of seeing entrepreneurs live lives that are a bunch of lies, I look at the concept of wealth with such a skeptical eye."

Phil went on to explain that, more than just hiding the truth of their financial situations, people aren't just kidding the world around them; they're kidding themselves. "I did a loan one time for a guy who had a car payment of forty-three hundred per month. He said to me, 'One day, when you're successful, you'll have a car payment like this.' I just smiled. This is what I'm supposed to aspire to? Everyone's perception of wealth is a joke."

It was with this skepticism that Phil walked into the first global entrepreneur meeting, and the second, and the third, hoping to connect with entrepreneurs who, like him, cared about the bottom line. As usual, all he heard was the same question over and over again. "How big is it?"

"All of the conversations were about revenue. Even the first conversation you and I had, Mike. It's bullshit. It's total bullshit," Phil said.

"Who cares about revenue? So you're running a twenty or fifty million-dollar company. You're living in a crap apartment, dude! You've got nothing in your accounts! The bank owns that car in the driveway. The credit card company owns your furniture. Your elderly parents paid for your vacation. Are you kidding me? What about profit? It makes no logical sense."

It's true. At our entrepreneur meetings there was little talk of profit, and many people in the room were counting on the sale of their businesses to finally cash in on their perceived success. When someone couldn't cover payroll that month, they would say they just needed one big project, or one new client, or an investor to swoop in. It's a common refrain among check-to-check entrepreneurs. One more big sale. One new client. Someone to just throw a lot of money at them.

These entrepreneurs were giving it everything they had to just survive, with one eye on the emergency exit sign.

I may not have been actively looking for an exit strategy while I ran my first two businesses, but it was the sale of those businesses that gave me actual wealth—and "permission" to act like an idiot. Would I have had the money to buy an expensive "stable" (yes, I used the obnoxious term) of cars and invest in poorly planned start-ups if I hadn't sold my business? Nope. It doesn't matter how much money you have coming in, if you're only focused on growth, you aren't going to have much to show for your "big" business.

The exit strategy you're banking on? It rarely happens. My experience was the exception, partly due to my being in the right place at the right time. Buyers, investors, vendors and clients, too, are attracted to healthy businesses. Strong businesses. But that seems to be a rarity nowadays. Doesn't it?

Top line thinking (focusing on income) goes way beyond business. It's definitely part of American culture, this emphasis on size. Bigger is better. More, more, more. Grow! Grow! Grow! Heck, I even wrote a book about how to do it.

As I said in the introduction to *The Pumpkin Plan,* I stand by my method for growing niche-dominating businesses that lead to giant success. But we can't sustain that growth—or enjoy the fruits of our labors—if we keep putting profit at the bottom of our to-do list. Are you really going to keep struggling as you wait for that one big sale, that one big contract, that one big payoff that will erase all of your debt, get you back in the black and allow you to finally cut yourself a big fat check? It rarely happens and, when it does, the money seems to evaporate fast. It's a bit like asking Santa Claus for a million dollars, knowing full well that he's just a drunk guy in a red suit working at the mall (and for God's sake get off his lap).

I say we start a movement, right here and right now, to replace that tired old misguided question about size and replace it with this one: "How healthy is your business?" I'm serious—I can envision that question on t-shirts, hats, maybe someone (hint: you, not me) even tattooing a questionable area of his body with the slogan. Better yet, how about a blimp flying over Wall Street? That's how big a deal this is.

If you spend one more second worrying about the size of your business while compromising a strong bottom line, your business is unhealthy at best. More likely your business is dying a slow death. Big business is great, but only if there are healthy profits. Small is great too, but only if there are healthy profits. Medium is great, but only if there are profits there, too. You get the picture, Goldilocks.

So, from this very second forward, ask only one question of yourself. Ask only one question of your entrepreneurial friends. Ask only one question of any business owner.

How *healthy* is your business?

Are you eating first, or are you surviving on leftovers, or worse—scraps from the garbage can in the alley?

By the end of this chapter, you'll answer that question; and whether your business is dying or just a little queasy, we are going to get it back to full health. I don't care how much your business is struggling financially, the fact that you are still in business means we can turn it around. Now, when people ask you how business is going, you will respond with, "Healthy. Things are very, very healthy!" And you won't be lying to them or yourself. You can even get naked to prove it.

THE (ALMOST) INSTANT ASSESSMENT

Whether your business is simply not as profitable as you would like it to be or is in full cardiac arrest, I need you to be willing to keep your eyes wide open. In order for Profit First to work, you need to come to this with no blinders on.

As you complete the Instant Assessment, remember that different businesses have different setups. I'll help you get to the perfect numbers for your specific business in the next chapter. For now, know that, while the numbers I provide in this chapter are ballpark numbers, they are a surprisingly effective way to get started, and you may be surprised at how accurate this Instant Assessment really is.

Figure 3 is the Profit First Instant Assessment form. Complete the form right now! You can write right in this book (or, if you are on an iPad or Kindle or some other reader and don't want to replace the screen, you can download a printable copy from the Resources section at Mike Michalowicz.com.)

1. In the Actual column, enter your Top Line Revenue for the last twelve full months. This is your total revenue, and

	ACTUAL	PF%	PF$	THE BLEED	THE FIX
Top Line Revenue					
Material & Subs					
Real Revenue		100%			
Profit					
Owner's Pay					
Tax					
Operating Expenses					

Figure 3: Profit First Assessment Form

you should be able to pull this number directly from your accounting system.

2. If you are a manufacturer or retailer, or if most of your sales are derived from the resale or assembly of inventory, put the cost of materials (not labor) for the last twelve full months in the Material & Subs cell.

3. If subcontractors deliver most of your services, put the cost of the subcontractors for these twelve months in the Material & Subs cell. (Subcontractors are people who work for you, but have the ability to work autonomously and to work for others. You don't pay them on payroll, you pay them their project fee, commission or hourly rate, and they handle their taxes, benefits, etc. themselves.) In some cases you will have both materials and subcontractor costs (think home construction). In that case, put the cumulative amount of these two costs in the Material & Subs cell. Remember to only put your materials and subcontracts here, but not labor costs for your own people.

4. If you are a service company and most of your services are provided by your employees (you included), put an n/a symbol in the Material & Subs section.

5. Now subtract your Material & Subs number from your Top Line Revenue to calculate your Real Revenue. If you put an n/a in the Material & Subs section, just copy the Top Line Revenue number to the Real Revenue cell.

6. The goal is to get you to your Real Revenue number. This is the real money your company makes. For the other stuff—subs, materials, etc.—you may make a margin, but it isn't the core driver of profitability because you have little control over it. This can be a real wake-up moment for entrepreneurs. That real estate agency that does $5,000,000 in annual revenue and has a couple dozen agents (subcontractors) taking $4,000,000 in commissions is really a $1,000,000 business that manages real estate agents making $4,000,000, not a $5,000,000 business. The $3,000,000 a year staffing firm that bills out subcontractors to do work, and pays those subs $2,500,000, is really a $500,000 business. The accounting firm that bills out $2,000,000 in annual fees and has an in-house staff that does almost all the work has Real Revenue of $2,000,000 a year. The Real Revenue number is a simple, fast way to put all companies on equal footing (their Real Revenue numbers).

Real Revenue is different from Gross Profit, in that Real Revenue is your Total Revenue minus materials and subcontractors used to create and deliver the service or product. Gross Profit is Total Revenue minus materials, subcontractors and any of your employee's time used to create and deliver the service or product. It is a subtle difference but a critically important one. Gross Profit includes a portion of your employees' time. But the thing is this: You will generally pay your employees for their time whether you have a bad sales day or a good one. You will likely pay them the same salary if they fix a car transmission in four hours or five. So, to simplify things, we categorize any employee that you have, full or part time, as a cost of the business operations, not as a cost of the good sold.

7. Now that we know your Real Revenue, write down your actual profit from the last twelve months in the Profit cell. This is the cumulative profit you have sitting in the bank, or have distributed to yourself (and/or partners) as a bonus on top of—but not to supplement—your salary. If you think you have a profit but it is not in the bank and was never distributed to you as a bonus, this means you don't really have a profit. (If it turns out that you have less profit than you thought you would, it's likely you used it to pay down debt from previous years. Or maybe you are attempting an Enron re-make.)

8. In the Owner's Pay cell, put down how much you paid yourself (and any other owners of the business) these past twelve months in regular payroll distributions, not profit distributions.

9. In the Tax cell, put down how much money you have paid in taxes over the last twelve months, plus any money you have already reserved for taxes.

10. In the Operating Expenses cell, add up the total expenses you paid for the last twelve months—everything except your profits, owner's pay, taxes and any materials and subs that you have already accounted for.

11. Double-check your work by adding up your profit, owner's pay, taxes and operating expenses to see if you get your Real

Revenue number. If you don't get this number, something is wrong with your calculations. Go fix it. Then, add your Real Revenue to the Material & Subs costs and you should get the Top Line Revenue number. Make sure it all squares out.

12. Next, enter the profit percentage in the PF % column based upon your Real Revenue Range. Use the percentages in Figure 4. I call these percentages TAPs (Target Allocation Percentages), the percentage of each deposit that will be allocated to different elements of our business.

   For example, if your Real Revenue for the last twelve months is $722,000, you should use column C. If your business has $225,000 in Real Revenue, use Column A. If you run a division (or have your own company) that does $40,000,000, use column F.

13. In the PF $ column, copy the Real Revenue number from your actual column. Then multiply that Real Revenue number by the PF % for each row and write down the number in the corresponding PF $ cell. These are your

	A	B	C	D	E	F
Real Revenue Range	$0 – $250K	$250K – $500K	$500K – $1M	$1M – $5M	$5M – $10M	$10M – $50M
Real Revenue	100%	100%	100%	100%	100%	100%
Profit	5%	10%	15%	10%	15%	20%
Owner's Pay	50%	35%	20%	10%	5%	0%
Tax	15%	15%	15%	15%	15%	15%
Operating Expenses	30%	40%	50%	65%	65%	65%

Figure 4: Target Allocation Percentages (TAPs)

target PF dollar amounts for each category. Welcome to the moment of truth. (I hope we can still be friends.)

14. In the Bleed column, take your Actual number and subtract the PF $ number. This is very likely to result in a negative number. It is your bleed, the amount you need to make up. Negative means you are bleeding out money in these sections. Sometimes it is in just one category with a problem, but in most cases businesses are bleeding out in the Profit, Owner's Pay and Tax Accounts and have a positive number (meaning excess) in Operating Expenses. In other words, we are paying too little in profit, owner salaries, and taxes, and paying too much in operating expenses.

15. In the final column, The Fix, put either "increase" or "decrease" next to each category. If the number in the Bleed section is a negative number, put "increase" in the corresponding Fix cell, because we need to increase our contribution to this category to correct the Bleed. Conversely, if it is a positive number in the Bleed section, put "decrease" in the Fix cell, since this is a category where we need to spend less money in order to fix it.

Figure 5 is a completed example from a law firm to which I just introduced this process: The Instant Assessment reveals a few (painful) things. This business is not nearly profitable enough—it should be filling the profit coffers by $118,000 more every year. At $5,000 in the Profit Account, this is basically a break-even business. One bad month and this company is going down.

The two owners are taking a combined salary of $190,000, which is way too much for a business of this size. The owners are likely living a bigger lifestyle than the business can afford, and they need to cut their salaries by $67,000.

As the business gets healthier, the taxes will increase. (More taxes, as painful as they are to pay, are a sign of a healthy business—the

	ACTUAL	PF%	PF$	THE BLEED	THE FIX
Top Line Revenue	$1,233,000				
Material & Subs	N/A				
Real Revenue	$1,233,000	100%	$1,233,000		
Profit	$5,000	10%	$123,000	($118,000)	Increase
Owner's Pay	$190,000	10%	$123,000	$67,000	Decrease
Tax	$95,000	15%	$184,950	($89,950)	Increase
Operating Expenses	$943,000	65%	$801,450	$141,550	Decrease

Figure 5: Completed Instant Assessment for Law Firm

more you make, the more you pay... until you make so much you lobby politicians and pay nothing. Don't get me started.) And those Operating Expenses are too high, to the tune of more than $141,000.

Looking at this Instant Assessment, it's obvious what this company's leaders need to do to make their business healthy: Cut owners' salaries and cut operating costs, possibly including staff. It will require courage, and it is going to be painful.

The Instant Assessment brings clarity fast, and it can be a rude awakening. No more putting things off. No more hoping that big client, big check or big anything will save you from the day-to-day panic. We know exactly what we need to do.

A financially healthy company is a result of a series of small daily financial wins, not one big moment. Profitability isn't an event; it's a habit.

WHY PERCENTAGES?

What if I told you I knew of a successful bikini model and fitness trainer who weighs 205 pounds? You would assume she was seriously overweight, right? How could she be a bikini model? Easy. She's six foot eight! Amazon Eve is the tallest bikini model in the world and, I'm telling you, she's ripped. (Google her.) Her weight is ideal for her height. Fitness is relative. Health is relative. So are numbers.

In this book I use the phrase "top line" thinking, which is when you focus on revenue, revenue first and foremost, with profit as an afterthought. Top line thinking is dangerous because numbers are relative. You may have a million in revenue, but that's a whole lot of nothing if your expenses and debt load is also seven figures. At $500K you might view your top line as meager compared to other businesses in your industry, but if you're pulling in eighty percent in pay and profit, that is far from meager. That's gorgeous. Super model gorgeous. And if your business is showing fifty million in revenue, but pulling in two percent in pay and profit, that's ugly, my friend. Frankenstein, ugly. (And we all know how ugly that is.) So, rather than focus on actual numbers alone, look at percentages. Percentages show the relationship, giving you an accurate picture of what's really happening with your business.

HOW DID I DETERMINE THESE NUMBERS AND PERCENTAGES?

These are typical ranges that I have found while working with countless companies over the years and in running my own. The percentages aren't perfect, but they are an excellent starting point. And they represent what I have found to be very healthy numbers. But here is the deal—they may not work for you perfectly, but that is okay because these percentages are your target, what you will move toward. We are going to move in small steps. More on that soon, but here are the deets behind the percentages.

When a company is doing less than $250,000 in revenue it typically has one employee: you. You are the key employee and usually the only employee (with some contractors, part-timers, or maybe possibly one full-timer). Many freelancers are at this stage and if they elect to stay there (just them and no employees) they should be able to increase the profit and pay percentages even more than what I have listed, because they don't have the expense of employees or the need to incur the expenses necessary to support multiple employees.

At $250K to $500K, you likely have employees. Basic systems will be necessary (like a shared CRM for your team), equipment, etc., plus you will need to pay your people, so operating expenses increase. Owner's Pay adjusts down (and will continue to) as you take your first step in being a little less employee and a little more shareholder, when other people start to do the work, and you get the benefit of the profits via your distributions.

At $500K to $1M, the growth trend and patterns continue with more systems and more people. Focus on increasing profits because, for so many businesses, the growth from $1M to $5M is the hardest. You want a little reserve.

From $1M to $5M, systems are no longer added because they are nice to have; now systems become absolutely mandatory. You can't keep it all in your head any more. Often the biggest investment into the business needs to happen at this time, as all the knowledge in your head needs to be converted to systems and processes and check lists. This means larger allocations must be put toward Operating Expenses. This is when you are no longer doing most of the work; this is when, if your business is to grow, a significant portion of your time is spent working on the business (not in it), and the rest of your time is spent selling the big projects.

At $5M to $10M, typically a management team enters a company to bring it to the next stage, and a clear second tier of management starts to form. The founder starts more and more to focus on her special strengths. The owner is on a consistent payroll, and the majority of her take home income is from the profitability of the company, not the salary she takes.

At $10M to $50M, a business will often stabilize and achieve predictable growth. The founder's income is almost entirely made up of profit distributions. Owners' salaries are relative to their roles, but typically are insignificant. Businesses of this size can leverage efficiency in big ways to maximize profitability.

RUDE AWAKENING

You might remember that during my "rebuilding" period, I wrote my first book, *The Toilet Paper Entrepreneur;* the foundation of which was a series of principles I used to start my businesses. Chief among these principles was frugality—I wholeheartedly believed that any entrepreneur could start a business with little or no seed money and grow that business no matter what they had in the bank. The book is full of tips for saving money while launching and running a business, and since its publication I've heard from thousands of entrepreneurs who followed the advice (or a variant thereof) while starting or operating their own businesses.

And let me tell you, I didn't just spout off about frugality. After my spending craze, after my come-to-Jesus moment (if Jesus were named "near bankruptcy"), I went back to my roots. Way back. Not because I had to, this time, but because I wanted to. I made it my mission to get what I needed for my business on the cheap and took pride in doing so. My office space cost a mere $1000 per month—peanuts compared to my previous $14,000 a month digs. I got my gently-used conference room furniture for a whopping 75% discount. My dry erase board was homemade, with white board material used in showers, dental floss and some car wax. (Top that, MacGyver!)

So imagine my surprise when I ran my own assessment on my business and discovered that, despite my frugal superpowers, I was still bleeding out. It is not an exaggeration to say I was shocked to discover this. "How much cheaper can I get this stuff?" I thought, beyond frustrated.

Then I realized—duh. It wasn't how *much* I was spending on expense line items. The problem was, I shouldn't have been spending *anything* on some of those line items. For example, I didn't really need an office space. I wasn't seeing clients or greeting customers. I was writing a book and building a speaking career, which meant I spent a lot of time alone, on the road and in phone and Skype meetings. My subcontractors could just as easily do their work from home.

Truth was, I *wanted* an office space because it made me feel legitimate. And let me tell you, after my piggy bank moment,

I needed to feel that. But the bottom line was, I couldn't keep it up if I wanted to turn a profit every month. So I sublet my office space and found a sweet deal at a cookie factory—free office and meeting space from a trusted, long-time friend. I cut expense line items across the board until I stopped the bleeding and watched my business and profit grow. An added bonus was free cookies. And when I say added bonus, I mean it added about five pounds around my waist. So… not really a bonus, after all.

For some people, the Instant Assessment brings about a rude awakening that is far more devastating than mine. I'd already been through the wringer, so realizing I had to cut a few line items was a shock, but not a big deal. Cutting cost has become almost enjoyable. It has become strategic in a way. How can I achieve the same or better with less or no cost? For Debbie Horovitch, whose story I shared with you in the introduction, the rude awakening led to a near-breakdown with a total stranger (me—so, you know, a "very handsome young man," according to my mom). It led to Debbie feeling like a fool.

I have applied the Instant Assessment to countless businesses, and the reactions vary from, "Really? I can do that?" to "Who the hell do you think you are, Mike, telling me where my business should be? You know nothing about my unique industry!" to buckling knees and tears streaming down people's faces. It's hard to face the harsh reality that your business is worse off than you thought it was. But now you know, and knowledge is power. Now we can fix it.

You are not a fool. You have done nothing wrong, and you have nothing to be ashamed of. You have this book in your hands. You are discovering the truth and another way to get where you want to go. You are no longer asking, "How can I make my business bigger?" You are asking, "How can I make my business healthier?"

WHAT IF YOUR BUSINESS IS BRAND NEW

How does Profit First work if you just launched your business and have no revenue? Should you wait until you have some to start using

Profit First? Heck, no. Starting with squat, with your whole business future ahead of you is actually the best time to start using Profit First. Why? Because it allows you to form a powerful habit right from the get-go, when your business is forming and, perhaps more importantly, prevents you from developing bad financial habits that can be difficult to break.

A baby is a poor indication of what a person will look like as an adult; the same is true for a brand new business. You may end up serving a different type of client than you plan to serve right now. I suspect the founder of Ugg, who initially made the popular line for surfers, never imagined teenage girls would become his primary market. Also, in the early stages of building a business, you need to spend as much time as possible on the selling and the doing; systems and processes come later. For these reasons, it's best not to worry about getting the exact right percentages for your business.

Simply use the percentages in the Instant Assessment for your target allocations, but start at 1% allocation for the Profit Account, 50% for Owner's Pay and 15% for the Tax Account. Use quarterly adjustments to step up to higher percentages and nudge your business closer to the TAPs recommended in this book. And as for the advanced Profit First strategies I share in the end of the book—don't worry about any of that until your business has been active for at least a year. The goal for new businesses is to form the basic core good Profit First habit and then spend every other waking second getting your baby off the ground.

ACTION STEP
COMPLETE THE INSTANT ASSESSMENT

Step 1 (the one and only step): This entire chapter is really one big action step, so if you have not yet completed an Instant Assessment on your business, do it now. Can you get a lot out of this book if you table this exercise for when you have more time or feel up to facing reality? Sure. Will you get the most out of reading this book and see results quickly if you don't? Nope. So stop right now and do it.

PLEASE READ THIS NOW

If you are feeling overwhelmed, bad about yourself and the choices you've made, or angry about the numbers you came up with in your Instant Assessment, there is something I want you to know:

You are normal.

If you are having trouble facing the rest of this book, that's okay. Stop now and come back to it when you feel ready to face it. But do this one thing: set up a Profit Account at a separate bank and, every time you make a deposit, move one percent into that account. I know it's "peanuts" and you may think the amount is too small to make an impact on your business, but that is the reason you're going to keep the profit allocation percentage low. You can run your business as you always have, and you won't feel a thing, but you will start the habit that will change your business forever. Soon enough, the feeling of being overwhelmed, the anger and frustration, will fade as your new profit habit builds. Then you can crack this book again and dig in to the rest of the Profit First system.

CHOOSE YOUR OWN ADVENTURE

W HEN I was a kid, I loved reading *Choose Your Own Adventure* books (and quite frankly, I'll still dig into an R.A. Montgomery book if it crosses my path). You know, the interactive books with a message at the end of each chapter that says something like: "If you want to take the path through the woods, turn to page 51. If you want to take the boat, turn to page 80."

Here's your chance to relive a part of your childhood—you get to choose which Profit First adventure you want to have next. The only difference between this and the classic *Choose Your Own Adventure* books is, no matter which page you turn to, as long as you follow the Profit First system you will be victorious. Simply choose a path that fits your needs right now. But whichever path you choose, the ending is the same no matter what: perpetual profit.

Let's get to it. Time to pick your direction in your adventures in profit. You put your sword back in its sheath. You raise your torch high, illuminating the room. A large pile of cash sits in front of you, ready for the taking. You choose what happens next:

1. You are the type who wants to continue on with this adventure, now. So you quickly scoop up the pile of cash, stuff it into your backpack and draw your sword, ready for the next challenge. (If you want to start implementing Profit First right this second using your Instant Assessment percentages, turn to Chapter 5.)

2. You are the type who accounts for the details. Is that a black widow spider crawling amongst the bills? And what's that

slimy, slithering thing peering at you from the corner of the room? Is it a snake—or worse, an IRS agent?

You carefully count and stack every single dollar, write out a receipt and place the money securely in your backpack. The next adventure will surely present itself, but for now you'll cross every T and dot every I. (If you want to master the nuances of the Instant Assessment and come up with percentages that are perfectly suited to your business, then continue reading this chapter.)

Note: There are a lot of numbers in this chapter. If you choose option 2 and make it through this chapter alive, tweet me a selfie.

There is no wrong choice. You may want to jump right in and come back later to tweak your percentages. Or you may want to come up with a customized assessment so that you don't *have* to come back later. Either way, as long as you're actually working the Profit First system, you're winning.

GETTING DOWN TO THE NITTY-GRITTY

The Instant Assessment is based on ranges. Every business is slightly different (though your business and your industry are not nearly as unique as you may think). The numbers you came up with in the Instant Assessment won't be perfect, but they are probably close to what you'll end up with after a more detailed assessment.

Before we dig in, I want to address two common problems entrepreneurs face when they decide to start following the Profit First system—and they do not go hand in hand.

First, some entrepreneurs make the mistake of getting trapped in the details, spending hours, days, weeks or longer perfecting their percentages before they *do* anything. Worse, some entrepreneurs who get stuck in the minutiae never get around to doing anything. It's our old nemesis: analysis paralysis. In this chapter, we get down to the nitty-gritty; but if at any time you think you are lost in a research and percentage-tweaking rabbit hole, stop and move on to the next chapter. Perfectionism kills every dream—better to just start.

On the other hand, if you're like me, you might make the common mistake of taking action too big and too fast. I'm the type who starts before I have all of the information because most of the learning occurs in the doing, anyway. But I put success at risk when I go into a situation ill-prepared. In those cases, my ego blames the system when mistakes were simply due to the fact that I didn't put in the necessary preparation.

I've seen entrepreneurs kickstart their Profit First system by taking a profit percentage of twenty percent immediately. They say, "This is so simple. I get it. Bammo! Twenty percent! I'm done. Next problem."

Not so fast, Chiefy. This is a classic mistake, one I've made myself. Going full-throttle Profit First on the first day is like donating five gallons of blood at your first blood drive. You know what would happen if you tried to do that? You would die. The body has less than two gallons of blood pumping through it, so you'd keel over way before you reached your five-gallon goal anyway. However, there is a way to reach that goal in a safe way. If we donate small amounts over time, eventually we will donate five gallons—cumulatively.

If you hoard most of the food at the table, you're not leaving any fuel for your business. Remember, your business, not you, is now living off of the leftovers. So make sure the share you take leaves enough for your business to continue to thrive. Rather than go with one extreme—too slow or too fast—let's just meet somewhere in the middle.

The key to successful Profit First implementation lies in stringing together a series of many small steps in a repeating pattern. So take it easy.

While you slowly start to build up your Profit First muscle, we are also going to get you into a simple, repeating pattern. All music has a rhythm. Rhythm is what moves the music forward, and moves you. Otherwise it would just be random noise, and you would never be moved by it. Entrepreneurs typically manage their money in an erratic, noisy rhythm that causes confusion and panic. But by the end of the next chapter, we will get you into a simple rhythm that will give you clarity and control over your financials.

Let's dig in.

YOUR PROFIT TARGET ALLOCATION PERCENTAGES (TAPS)

The Instant Assessment is a starting point for all of your Target Allocation Percentages (TAPs). TAPs are the goals we have set to distribute to each account based on percentages. We may want to ultimately be tucking away 20% of our accumulated deposits; if so, 20% would be the TAP for Profit. We won't necessarily start there, but we will build to it.

Now you need to do a little bit of research to set more specific target numbers. There are a few ways to approach this:

1. Research public companies: Look at the financial reports public companies are required to make available. Do a quick Internet search using the term "financial market overview" and you will find dozens of websites that report the financials for public companies. Look up at least five companies in your industry, or a similar industry. If you don't find your niche, try expanding. For instance, if you find no public DJ companies, expand to entertainment companies and select five that come close. (Tip: My preference is Marketwatch.com for these reports, because the site is easy to navigate. You might also try Yahoo! Finance and Google Finance.)

    For our purposes, look up the income statements for the last three to five years. If you really want to dig in, check out the balance sheets and cash flow statements for these companies, too.

    For each year, divide the net income (profit) number by the total sales/revenue number. Do this for each year and then come up with the average. This is how you find the profit percentage for any public company. Do this for each of the five public companies you look at, and you will find the overall industry profit average.

Use that overall industry profit average as your Profit TAP.

2. Review your tax returns for the last three to five years and determine your most profitable year (based on percentages, not on dollar amounts). Why do we want the percentage? Because a billion-dollar company that only reports a million dollars in profit is in big trouble. Even if they only had one bad day, a million bucks wouldn't be enough to bail them out. But a five million-dollar company that reports a million in profits is kicking butt and taking names. That lil' ol' company spits at bad days.

3. Or, the easiest way, just pick your profit percentage number based on your projected revenue for this year, using revenue for the last twelve months from the Instant Assessment form you filled out for Chapter 3. (You did fill it out, right?) Remember, the form is also available for free download in the Resources section at MikeMichalowicz.com.

If more than half the stuff your company sells comes from materials rather than labor or software—as happens with manufacturers, restaurants and retailers—use the gross profit (sometime called gross income) as the Real Revenue number. Gross profit is calculated somewhat similarly to how I suggest you determine your Real Revenue, and you need to evaluate your business based on that. Whenever you run the numbers for your business, or evaluate others, you will always base it on Real Revenue (gross profit).

Since at this point your Profit Account will fund your profit distributions and serve as your rainy day fund, you'll want your Profit Percentage to grow past five percent quickly. If you save five percent of your company's annual income, for example, that represents about twenty-one days of operating cash, which would help you keep your business afloat if your income were to plummet. (If your income dried up, you would stop contributing to your Profit Account and Tax Account and stop profit distributions to owners.) Three weeks is not much time to fix the problem, but Armageddon rarely happens. More often, revenue slows down over time, and you'll have at least something coming in during lean times. Kinda like a "Hangnail-ageddon" instead of an Armageddon. (It's a bad joke, I know, but I like it. So it stays.)

If your sales were to stop completely, with not a single deposit coming in, here's a good longevity rule of thumb:

1. 5% profit allocation = 3 weeks of operating cash

2. 12% profit allocation= 2 months of operating cash

3. 24% profit allocation = 5 months of operating cash.

Why is it that, as the PF percentages basically double, longevity almost triples? The math doesn't seem to make sense at first glance. But it does make sense. The bigger your PF percentage, the more efficiently you are running your business, which means less in operating expenses. So not only do you have more saved up with a higher PF percentage, you spend less, which affords you even more time.

The goal is to make your PF as high as possible. However, super-high profit percentages are not sustainable. At least not for long, and definitely not if your revenue stays stagnant. The reason for this is, if you can pull off consistently fat profits—say 50% allocated to your Profit Account—and your Operating Expenses Account for only 10% of revenue, your competitors will figure out what you're doing. Then, to get more business, they will drop prices (they likely have the profit margins to afford it). When that happens, you will have to drop prices too in order to stay in business. For competitive sharks, fat margins can be like blood in the water. The only way to keep big margins is to milk them for all they're worth when you have them and keep innovating to find new ways to bump up profitability.

OWNER'S PAY TAPS

Gone are the days when you paid everyone but yourself and had to support your life with credit cards and loans from the in-laws. Remember, your business is supposed to serve you; you are not in service to your business! No more leftovers for you!

Owner's Pay is the amount you and the other equity owners take in pay for the work you do. (Equity members of your company who do not work in the business just get a profit distribution.) Your salary should be on par with the going rate for the work you do, in other words—the salary you would have to pay your replacement.

There are two options to consider when choosing your Owner's Pay TAPs number. Either:

1. Take a realistic look at the work you do. If you have a small company with, say, five employees, you may call yourself the CEO—but that's just the title on your card. Likely, you are doing a lot of other work. You probably spend a lot of time selling, completing projects, handling customers and dealing with HR concerns. In reality, around two percent of your time is spent actually doing the job of CEO—vision planning, strategic negotiations, acquisitions, reporting to investors, addressing the media, etc. Determine your salary based on what you are doing 80% of the time, and what you would reasonably pay employees to do those jobs.

2. Evaluate pay for all equity owners who work in the business. Add up the salaries that represent your Owner's Pay draw. The percentage of revenue must, at minimum, cover Owner's Pay draw. Remember, you will likely get raises—maybe even a bonus for a job well done. So make the percentage one-and-a-quarter times the amount you determine for your salaries, so you can adjust for revenue fluctuations.

Or, pick the percentage I suggested in the Instant Assessment, based on your revenue range. (Refer to Figure 4.) The money that is transferred into this account is divided among all equity employees. It does not have to be split up equally, nor does it have to be split up based on your equity percentages.

Why should you have a separate account if you and the other equity owners working in the business are just employees? Because you are the most important employee. If you had to fire people, I suspect you would fire everyone else before you fired yourself. Think about your very best employee. I'll bet you take extra steps to ensure that you are taking care of her. I'll bet you would do everything in your power to keep your best employees happy, including paying them what they're worth, right? Well guess what, Bucko! *You* are your best, most important employee. We must take care of you.

When it comes to pay, different business formations require you to take Owner's Pay in different ways. An S-Corp is treated differently than an LLC or a sole proprietorship, which are both treated way differently than a C-Corp. The Owner's Pay allocation still works the same way; you just need to work with your accountant to make sure the money flows out properly and legally. (I strongly recommend an accountant who is a certified Profit First Professional, meaning they get this and know exactly how to support your Profit First business.)

WHEN YOUR CURRENT PAY IS LESS THAN THE ASSESSMENT

I was having dinner with my friend Rodrigo when he told me how his business generated $350,000 in annual revenue, but he was living on below-minimum wage.

As a thunderstorm approached in the distance, I took the napkin with the least amount of salsa stains and jotted down Rodrigo's numbers. Multiplying his $350,000 in Real Revenue by 35% (from the Instant Assessment), I came up with just over $122,000.

"How many partners work in the business?" I asked.

"Me, and one other," he replied.

Dividing by two, the amount for owner's pay was a little over $61,000 each, but that was if they were doing the same work, warranting a fifty-fifty split. As we discussed in the previous section, owner's pay should represent the work you do.

When I asked Rodrigo for more details about his own pay, he said, "I take roughly $30,000 a year, and my partner left to get a full-time job, so he takes zero now. We have three full-time employees at $65,000 each per year, and I manage them."

I'd like to say I was shocked, but this scenario is all too common. I did wonder how Rodrigo was supporting himself and his family on below-minimum wage. I figured he was using credit cards, family loans and possibly a home re-finance to supplement his paltry income.

"If all three of your employees decided to leave on the same day, what would you do?" I asked.

"I would do all of the work myself and my partner would come back."

"So why don't you do that?" I asked.

"Because then I would be stuck doing the work and it would not be able to grow," Rodrigo explained. "I don't want to do the work; I want to grow the business."

Rodrigo had the right idea, but he was executing it in the wrong way.

In *The E-Myth Revisited,* the classic must-read book by Michael Gerber, Michael explains that we should work *on* our business, not *in* it. (Yes, I call him Michael. We are friends. He calls me Mike and I call him Michael. And occasionally I call him Mike and he calls me Michael. And then we both get confused and start talking to ourselves.)

This "on vs. in" philosophy is spot-on, and yet most entrepreneurs have trouble executing it. Working *on* the business does not mean hiring a bunch of people to do the work and then spending all the livelong day answering their never-ending questions about how to do the job (the job you used to do). Shifting to a managerial role just means you are working *in* your business in a different way—and that you have a mongo payroll to cover every two weeks.

Working *on* your business is about building systems. Period. An entrepreneur is someone who finds the solutions to opportunities and problems and then builds systems to consistently deliver those solutions through other people or things.

However, what Rodrigo and so many entrepreneurs miss is that growing a company is not an overnight switch from doing all of the work to none of the work. The transition from working *in* the business to working *on* the business happens over time—slowly, deliberately, one small step followed by another small step. (Are you starting to see the theme here?) This is the reasoning behind the Owner's Pay percentages in the Instant Assessment—larger percentages for owners when the company is tiny and smaller percentages as the company grows.

In the early days of a company, when annual revenues are below $250,000, you are not only the most important employee; you are likely the *only* employee. If your annual revenue is under $500,000 and you have an employee or two, you are still the key employee. And that means you must be doing 90% of the work. You're bringing home the bacon and frying it up in the pan.

The other 10% of the time you spend documenting everything you do so that you can systematize it for your other few employees or contractors to do the work without your input. Basically, you are a true entrepreneur (building systems) 10% of the time, and a hardworking, hard-selling employee of your own company 90% of the time.

This is why you get such a big salary in the beginning. No more of this "bottom of the bowl" stuff. You can't live on minimum wage or less. Say it again, once more with feeling: *My business serves me; I do not serve my business.* Paying yourself next to nothing for hard work is servitude.

As your annual revenue grows past $500,000, you will transition to spending more time building systems. Now, you're a systems developer 20% of the time, a manager 10% of the time and an employee 70% of the time. (Note that the better you are at creating systems, the less management is required, because the recipe for how to things get done is consistent.)

As annual revenue grows past one million, your salary percentage will drop even farther because you will be working less and less *in* the business and more and more *on* the business.

However, remember that it is likely you will always work *in* your business. Because even if you are a master of building systems and spend 80% of your time in that magic zone, you'll still spend roughly 20% of your time handling the big sales. Almost every entrepreneur to CEO is in charge of the big sale. You bet your bottom dollar Jeff Bezos is in the room when Amazon is closing a hundred million-dollar deal. And when your big deals are on the table, you will be right there, sitting at its head.

Ironically, getting back *in* your business is the best way to create systems. And as you put the systems in place and your revenue increases to accommodate them, you can slowly plug in great people to implement those great systems.

The bottom line is this: Don't cut your salary to make the numbers work. The goal of every business is health, and that is achieved through efficiency. Your martyr syndrome is not doing anyone any favors; making yourself the sacrificial lamb does not promote efficiency, it hinders it.

YOUR TAX TAPS

Profit First is not about accounting to the exact penny (that's what your bookkeeper and accountant do). It is about handling your accounting quickly and easily, with numbers that are as close to accurate as possible. We work percentages off of the Real Revenue number and this is true for all your "small plate" accounts.

The first step in getting to your Tax TAP is to determine your income tax rate. Taxes range all over the place, depending on your amount of personal income and corporate profit and the area you live in. As of this writing, many entrepreneurs have an average income tax rate of 35% or so; for others it will be less, and in some countries is can be 60% or more.

When I traveled to Copenhagen, Denmark, the beauty of the country blew me away: the resources they have, and all the "free stuff"—the free healthcare, the free education (including universities), and the free-flowing confidence that they live in the best place in the world, which is kind of funny, because I always thought North Korea held that title.

Then my friend Lori Webb told me that the Danish tax rate is over 60%. I practically fell off my chair.

Taxes vary from country to country, income bracket to income bracket, and surely change everywhere every year (and, I think, in world history, never once in our favor). But regardless of what the numbers are, you need to prepare for them.

One goal of the Profit First system is that the company takes care of all forms of tax responsibility. It's mandatory that you talk with your accountant so she can advise you on all the ways you and your business will be taxed.

Here are four different approaches for determining your Tax TAP:

1. Look at your personal and business tax returns. Add up your taxes and then determine the percentage of taxes you paid compared to your Real Revenue. Do this again for the prior two years. Looking at your taxes as a percentage of Real Revenue for the last three years will give you a good sense of your ongoing tax responsibility.

2. From your accountant get your estimated tax responsibility for your business, year-to-date (YTD), and then determine your tax percentage of your YTD Real Revenue. Better yet, if your accountant is a certified Profit First Professional, she can simply tell you the percentage to reserve. (For a list of accountants, bookkeepers and other financial gurus who are Profit First Professionals, go to the Resources section at MikeMichalowicz.com.)

3. Do a search for "tax rates" + "your country" + "tax year." For example, "tax rates United States 2013" yielded the following results on Google:

Tax Rate Schedule Y-1, Internal Revenue Code section 1(a)
    10% on taxable income from $0 to $17,850, plus
    15% on taxable income over $17,850 to $72,500, plus
    25% on taxable income over $72,500 to $146,400, plus
    28% on taxable income over $146,400 to $223,050, plus
    33% on taxable income over $223,050 to $398,350, plus
    35% on taxable income over $398,350 to $450,000, plus
    39.6% on taxable income over $450,000.

Then, pick your likely income range—which depends on the type of company formation you may have and the combination of your Owner's Pay and Profit contributions—and you have your federal tax rate. Now do the same thing for state taxes and add the two.

4. Or simply use 35% as your tax number. It may not be perfect, but it's usually pretty effective. And while the optimal number will have you neither paying additional taxes at the end of the year nor receiving a refund, it is better to guess a little too high, get a refund and consider what to do with the extra cash than to get a call from your accountant, Keith, because you don't have enough money, and have to ask your daughter if you can borrow from her piggy bank. Trust me.

But hold on: If the tax rate is 35%, why would I only reserve 15% for taxes (as noted in the Instant Assessment I shared earlier)? Let's do a little simple math.

A LITTLE SIMPLE MATH

Now we are going to determine the percentage that stays in your Operating Expenses Account, after you move money to your Profit Account, your Owner's Pay Account and your Tax Account. The amount left over for expenses is likely going to be somewhere between 40% and 60%. This is the money you have available to pay all your expenses.

Next, subtract that percentage from 100%. So, if your total Operating Expenses Account is at 55%, you're left with 45%. That 45% is the amount you will be taxed on. (More often than not, expenses are not taxed. This is why some accountants encourage you to buy equipment or make other large purchases toward the end of the year.) Now, multiply your non-operating percentage (in this case, 45%) with your taxable income percentage (in this case, 35%). You end up with a percentage of approximately 16%, which is your Tax percentage.

Now that you have a more accurate picture of your actual percentages, you're ready to get started. In the next chapter we'll take you through the first year of Profit First, and beyond, and outline everything you need to know from day one. Congratulations! You survived. Send me a selfie.

I can sense your hunger to put this into practice in your business. Wipe that drool off your chin and let's start doing it. Things are about to change around here.

ACTION STEP
APPLY YOUR ADVANCED KNOWLEDGE

Step 1: Following the steps detailed above, determine your custom Profit, Owner's Pay and Tax percentages based on your industry and other factors.

Step 2: Since you chose to get down to the nitty-gritty and determine your exact Profit, Owner's Pay and Tax percentages, stop now and adjust the numbers in your Instant Assessment form.

DAY ONE, QUARTER ONE, YEAR ONE AND FOREVER
5

P ROFIT First works. Period. Whether you use the percentages I provided for you in the Instant Assessment or choose the path of assessing all the nuances of your business and industry (see Chapter 4) and arrive at your own perfect allocation percentages, it will work. How can it work with different percentages, you ask? Because your Target Allocation Percentages (TAPs) for your Profit, Owner's Pay and Tax Accounts are simply targets—you aren't going to start with them, you are going to build toward them. And as you build, you will transform your business into a lean, mean efficiency machine that generates profit on every deposit, no matter how small.

Remember, the Profit First formula flip is easy:

Sales – Profit = Expenses

If you're still stuck on finding your percentage, let me tell you a little story about the power of just doing it. This is a story I heard secondhand, maybe even seventeenthhand; I'm not sure. And while I don't know exactly whom the story is about, don't doubt the story. It goes like this:

An up-and-coming motivational speaker went to a speaking boot camp. During one of the sessions, the instructor explained how to make back-of-the-room sales. He said, "When you follow this method, eighty percent of the audience will buy your product at the end of an event."

With pages of notes and tons of enthusiasm, our up-and-comer set forth on the speaking circuit. Initially, she closed only 25% of her audiences. Reaching for that 80%, she tweaked and improved her strategy and pitch, constantly reviewing her notes. Over time her close rate rose to 50%, then 60%. After another year, she was consistently selling 75% of the room after her speech. She had achieved outstanding results, but not to the level her instructor had promised.

One morning, she sat down to breakfast with a few colleagues and her old instructor happened to be there. She couldn't wait to speak with him and get direction about what could help her get that last, elusive 5%. What was the secret to finally breaking 80%? When she told her story to her instructor, his jaw dropped.

"Eighty percent? You thought I said eighty percent? I said eighteen."

I tell you this story to illustrate something I believe to be true because I've experienced it—no matter what the number is, if you work toward it and believe it's a possibility, you will not only achieve it, you will blow past the "reasonable" numbers others have set.

If you made the detailed assessment in Chapter 4, you probably looked at quite a few public companies that are in the same space you are. You have seen their numbers. You have seen their "reasonable" 18%. That's my fear.

Even if you are following my guidelines and pushing for healthy profits of 15% or 20%, the number may be too low. Many companies have absolutely done better. Million-dollar companies have posted 40% or more in profits. Yes, they are the exception, but someone has to be. Why not you? Why not choose to hear 80% when the rest of the world chooses to hear 18%?

In this chapter, I will teach you exactly how to implement Profit First, step by step, day by day, month by month, and so on. Your Profit Percentage may seem steep or out of reach, but by the end of this year you will be closer to it than you thought you could be. You may even leave it in the dust.

BEFORE WE BEGIN, MEET THE PRIDE OF PROFIT FIRST

When Jorge Morales and Jose Pain started Specialized ECU Repair in 2007, they dreamed of one day enjoying what they perceived to be the big perk of owning a business: profit, or, extra money to spend on their own interests. (Jorge is really into free diving and Jose has a serious thing for model airplanes.)

Here's where many seasoned entrepreneurs chuckle knowingly under their breath because they think this Jorge and Jose are dreamers. Don't they know that entrepreneurship is about personal sacrifice? Unless they're exceptionally lucky, it will be a long time before they earn enough extra cash to indulge in their little hobbies… right?

Wrong.

Two years into operating their own business, Jorge and Jose had decided the only way they could reap the benefits of entrepreneurship would be to increase their salaries a little bit each year. (They were better off than most entrepreneurs in that they *did* have enough to pay their own salaries and hadn't fallen into the death trap of debt.)

Then they read the small section on Profit First Accounting in my book, *The Toilet Paper Entrepreneur,* and began applying the system almost immediately. Over the next few years, Jorge and Jose tweaked Profit First to suit their rapidly growing business, adjusting their Profit Account percentages and allowing Profit First to control that growth so that they never ended up underwater because of large purchases or a ridiculously high payroll.

Four years later Jorge and Jose have a thriving business that, in 2013, surpassed their accountant's revenue projections. Their staff has tripled, but thanks to their shrewd, careful planning and the Profit First system, they are not struggling under the weight of too-high operating expenses.

More importantly, their business is serving them, with salaries appropriate for their positions and the work they do at Specialized ECU Repair, and with significant Profit Account disbursements that have enabled them to live the lifestyle they envisioned when they started the business.

The dream all entrepreneurs have—that our business will *improve* the quality of our lives, not destroy it—Jorge and Jose are living that dream. They do not serve their business; their business serves *them.*

DAY ONE
TELL YOUR PEOPLE

Before you begin, I want you to tell your accountant what you're up to. A warning—he might not "get it." He may say the system is useless, or it won't work, or it's technically wrong or it's too much hassle. If your accountant discourages you from using Profit First in your business, it is because he does not fully understand cash flow management or human behavior. Get a new accountant.

Jorge and Jose included their financial professionals in the implementation of Profit First right from the start.

"When we first learned about Profit First, it made sense to us," Jorge told me, in one of our many phone calls about their progress. "I pulled the numbers and then, with our bookkeeper and accountant, we did a projection for the year. Then we worked in the Profit Account percentage we wanted to start with."

With buy-in from their accountant on the principles and processes of Profit First, Jorge and Jose have been able to systematically apply the method to their business with great success. Their accountant helps them meet their Profit First goals and stay the course.

To make your life easier, I have compiled a list of accountants, bookkeepers, financial planners and others certified as Profit First Professionals. They not only get Profit First, they use it for themselves and they use it with their existing clients. You can find the list on the Resources section at MikeMichalowicz.com. There you will also find a Profit First One-Sheet that gives a basic overview of the system so that all of your key financial staff/ vendors can get up to speed within a few minutes.

SET UP YOUR ACCOUNTS

If you didn't set up your accounts after reading Chapter 2 (shame on you), do so now. Most bank accounts allow you to assign a nickname to the account that is displayed, rather than just the account number. Give each account a name that is easy to identify and then put the percentage (or dollar amount—I'll explain that in Chapter 9) in the name in brackets. This makes running Profit First so much easier. For example:

OPERATING EXPENSES [45%] *8812
OWNER PAY [25%] *8833
PROFIT [15%] *8843
TAXES [15%] *8839

START OUT EASY

We are making progress now, baby! We have the accounts set up at your bank! Yippee. We have determined your TAPs. Now we're going to start with a manageable Profit Percentage that will allow us time to cut down on expenses and adjust to the new system.

We'll start at our historical contribution levels for each account and then add 1%. This may mean you start from zilch. If your business has never had a profit, or if you have sometimes had a profit and sometimes a loss, your profit has been zero. Therefore, our easy start for the Profit Account will be 1% (that's 0% historically plus 1%, starting today), and we will bump it up as we start getting into our quarterly rhythm.

If your taxes were usually 5% of your total revenue, we are going to set up your tax reserve at 6%. If your pay represented 20% of your income, we add 1% to your 20% and you have 21%. And so on. Even if our targets are much higher, we start with what we've got, plus 1%.

Why start with small percentages, when we likely could do more? The reason is, the primary goal here is to establish a new, automatic routine for you. I want the amounts to be so small you don't even "feel" them. The goal is to set up these automatic allocations immediately, and then adjust the percentages each quarter until we are aligned with our TAPs.

Practical to the core, Jorge and Jose started out with a modest Profit First percentage of 2%. (Because their decision was made more than four years ago, before I finessed this system, their number was not based on the "1% rule" I've just shared with you.) They chose an allocation of 2% because initially, Jorge was reluctant to begin implementing Profit First—even though he knew it made perfect sense.

"I think by going slowly, I was able to see how Profit First could work," Jorge explained. "What it really came down to was, I realized that at two percent, there was no excuse not try it. Because if your business can't afford to set aside two percent of your revenue, it's probably not a business worth pursuing."

Start slow. These percentages you set are your quarterly allocation percentages. We are going to use them for the rest of this quarter, whether the quarter begins next week or in ninety-one days.

PROFIT STARTING TODAY

You know the saying, "Today is the first day of the rest of your life." I love it. I absolutely love it. To me, it represents the profound realization that we can change our lives (and our businesses) in a moment. Now is the time. This very *moment* we will make a profit for your business, and we will be profitable every day going forward. Please don't just read this and move on to the next chapter. I want you to take action now.

Right now, this moment, look at your bank balance in your Operating Expenses Account. Then subtract any outstanding checks and payments you have from that account. Divide up the remainder into your accounts based upon your TAPs. For example, say you have $5,000 in your bank account, and you have $3,000 in checks and payments still waiting to clear. That means you have $2,000 currently available. Run your percentages on that $2,000 and move that money into the accounts.

Do you have any deposits to make today? If so, tally up the deposits, put them in the bank, and then *immediately* distribute the money to all the other accounts. Do this for every deposit going forward.

(Don't worry: you don't need to do this every single day, or many times a day, if you have lots of deposits. We are going to get you into a twice-a-month rhythm shortly that will make this process very manageable.)

OUR FIRST CELEBRATION

Congrats! And I am not saying that lightly. You've just taken a big step. This is likely the first time in your entire business life that you have deliberately accounted for your profit first. Before anything else, you made sure you addressed your profit, your personal income and your tax responsibilities. That's a big deal. And it is a big step to a very, very healthy business. Kudos to you.

SLICE EXPENSES

Now that we are moving money into our Profit, Owner's Pay and Tax Accounts, we need to get the money from somewhere. There are only two ways to do that: by increasing sales and by cutting expenses. Increasing sales is very doable (you did read *The Pumpkin Plan*, right?) and is the key for colossal profitable growth. But it takes time and it won't happen overnight. Cutting expenses is generally a very quick process and is usually very easy.

Jorge and Jose run their business based on what they can afford today, not what they hope to be able to afford someday. So sometimes they have to wait to hire someone or make a high-ticket purchase.

"When big expenses showed up," Jorge explained, "we would sit down and ask ourselves, 'Do we really need this?' If we determined it would hurt our profits at the end of the year, we didn't buy it."

We just accounted for at least 3% (1% in each of the Profit, Owner and Tax Accounts) of our income, so we need to cover that by cutting 3% from our expenses. To do that, I need you to print out two things:

1. All your expenses for the last twelve months.

2. Any recurring expenses: rent, subscriptions, Internet access, training, classes, magazines, etc.

Now add up all the expenses and then multiply that number by 10%. You must cut costs by 10%. Now! No ifs, ands or buts! So why cut by at least 10%, when we "only need 3%"? Because cutting costs doesn't mean the bills go away overnight. It may take a month or two to pay down balances owed on expenses we eliminate. More importantly, we need to start building cash reserves, because by the start of the next quarter, we are going to move another 3% to your Profit, Tax and Owner's Pay Accounts, and then another 3% the quarter after that. So we want to account for that money quickly.

You can easily find your first 10% in cuts by doing the following:

1. Cancel whatever you don't need to help your business run efficiently and keep your customers happy.

2. Negotiate every remaining expense, except payroll.

I share a lot more about cutting expenses in the coming chapters. You are about to become a frugal (not cheap) entrepreneur. You will learn to use only what you need and not be wasteful. You will pay fairly for what you use, but you will use less. And you are going to *love it*.

MONTH AFTER MONTH
THE 10/25 RHYTHM

You remember my friend Debra Courtright, the bookkeeper who helped bail her client out of sales tax hell? When I first taught her how to use Profit First with her clients, I drove to her office in Fairfield, New Jersey to spend the day going over all of the advanced strategies. Just an hour into our training day, she had not only mastered the concepts, she was on the phone with one of her clients, helping her set up a Profit Account.

I always have my mobile office with me (backpack with laptop, other electronic gadgetry and critical lifesaving essentials—like Milano cookies). So while Debra went over the basics with her client, I knocked out a few tasks on my to-do list. I knew I had some bills due, so I went into my online bank account, looked at the Operating Expenses Account and ensured that all of the disbursements were current. Yep—Profit Account was up to do date. Tax Account looked good. Owner's Pay Account—check. Other advanced accounts we'll discuss later in the book—all good. Now it was time to pay my bills from the Operating Expenses Account.

"What are you doing?" Debra asked, startling me.

I had no idea she was behind me, and I practically spit out my coffee. If you met Debra, you would never guess that she is a fully trained super-ninja or something. But she must be, because she has an ability to just appear next to you without you noticing. My tip? Avoid drinking any form of liquid when she's around; you will either gag on it or spit it all over the table when you look up and see super-ninja Debra clinging to the ceiling above you.

"I'm paying my bills," I replied.

"Why are you paying them today?"

Confused, I replied, "Um. . . because I have time, and they're due."

Debra said, "Well, that's not smart." (Ninjas don't mince words.)

"What do you mean?" I asked.

That's when Debra taught me the 10th and 25th cash flow rhythm— paying expenses twice a month, on the 10th and 25th. And that was the day the 10/25 Rhythm became integral to Profit First. Thanks, Debra! (If that is your real name.)

I implemented the process in my business immediately. I let the bills come in, and I deposited income, but that was it. I no longer did accounting when I had time, or when someone called to check and see if I'd received an invoice. I got into a rhythm. I did my accounting every 10th and 25th (or the business day prior, if the 10th or 25th fell on a weekend or holiday). I chose those days so my payments arrive by the 15th and the end of the month, when most bills are due. For our benefit we want to get into a rhythm of twice a month, and for our vendors benefit we want to make sure we pay them on time.

First, I tallied all the new deposits that had gone in over the last few weeks and did the Profit First allocations, moving money into each account. Then I tallied up all the bills and put them in the system.

A little bit of magic started to happen. I became less and less reactive about bills. I didn't immediately look at the bank account when I got a big bill and wonder why I spent so much, and when I could pay this one off. Instead I started to feel more in control. By looking at my bills and my deposits two times a month, on the same days each time, I could see a pattern. I noticed that 80% of my bills were due at the beginning of the month, and that few were due in the second half. And I saw how my deposits were pretty equally dispersed over the month.

I realized that I had many "small" recurring bills that added up to a lot of money and were unnecessary expenses. I started to see trends and understand my cash flow. I didn't start to stack bills, paying what I could and then putting the ones I didn't pay back in a stack. I started to manage bills and cancel unnecessary stuff. I started to pay bills on time. Every bill.

Liz Dobrinska, my graphics guru who designed my website and even the cover of this book, told me, "I don't know what happened, Mike, but you now pay on time every time. I wish all my customers were like you."

Before I started following Debra's advice, I paid Liz inconsistently. Sometimes I paid the bill the day it arrived. At other times, I sat on it for sixty or ninety days. It wasn't because I was trying to take advantage of her; I was simply in reactionary mode. My method of bookkeeping was not an effective way to understand my cash flow or to keep my critically important vendors happy. The 10/25 Rhythm changed all that.

Here's how to get started:

1. Deposit all revenue into your Operating Expenses Account.

2. Every 10th and 25th day of the month, transfer the total deposits from the prior two weeks to each of your "small plate" accounts based on your current allocation percentages. For example, let's say you have $10,000 in total deposits for the past two weeks. Based on the following example percentages, here's how you would allocate the $10,000:
   Operating Expenses 43% - $4,300
   Tax 15% - $1,500

Owner's Pay 30% - $3,000
Profit 12% - $1,200
Employee Pay ($750) - $0
Petty Cash ($50) - $0

3. Transfer the specific dollar amounts from the Operating Expenses Account to respective accounts. In this example, Employee Pay for $750 and Petty Cash for $50. The accounts will now look like:
    Operating Expenses 43% - $3,500
    Tax 15% - $1,500
    Owner's Pay 30% - $3,000
    Profit 12% - $1,200
    Employee Pay ($750) - $750
    Petty Cash ($50) - $50

4. Transfer the full account balances for both your Tax and Profit Accounts to the respective "no temptation" accounts at your second bank.

5. You have $3,000 in the Owner's Pay Account from which to pay yourself. Take only what you have allocated as your bi-weekly salary, and leave the rest to accumulate. For this example, we'll say your bi-weekly salary is $2,750. This would leave $250 in the account.

6. Pay your employees from the Employee Pay Account. For example, if you pay $675 this pay period, it would leave $75 in the account.

7. With the remaining $3,500 in the Operating Expenses Account, pay your bills.

Once you've done all that, the accounts would look like this:
    Operating Expenses 43% - $50

Tax 15% - $0
Owner's Pay 30% - $250
Profit 12% - $0
Employee Pay ($750) - $75
Petty Cash ($50) - $50

Profit and Tax money will be accumulating at your "no temptation" second bank. As new deposits come in, you will deposit them in the Operating Expenses Account, and on every future 10th and 25th you will repeat these same seven steps.

A big note here: There is a strong possibility that you will not have enough money in your accounts to do all this. If so, you've got a major wake-up call. When you don't have enough money left over to pay your bills, it is your business screaming at the top of its lungs, warning you that you can't afford the bills you are incurring. You are spending more money than your business can support. But don't panic. Later in the book I detail a process that will help you adjust to the 10/25 Rhythm as comfortably as possible. Even if you can't pay everything on the 10th and 25th, you must get into this rhythm, because it will allow you to get a sense for the flow and accumulation of money. A heart fills with blood and pumps it out, forming a heartbeat. The lifeblood of your business is money; it should flow in a rhythm like a heart, not in a random, panicked pump here and there when you have money.

QUARTER ONE
QUARTERLY DISTRIBUTION

The new quarter has arrived. Yippee! You are about to take your very first ever quarterly distribution check. That's right, baby. Your business is serving *you*, now. You are going to take a distribution check every quarter. Every ninety days, profit will be shared to you. This is where your Frankenstein monster starts to become a powerful, lovable beast and serves you a fine meal on a silver platter with a perfectly matched California Pinot Noir. Don't you just want to pinch those chubby cheeks?

The quarters of every year are as follows:

Quarter 1 – Jan 1 to March 31
Quarter 2 – April 1 to June 30
Quarter 3 – July 1 to September 31
Quarter 4 – Oct 1 to December 31

(This assumes your fiscal year is the same as the calendar year. If you have a funky fiscal year, like if your year-end is May 31st, then your quarters will be different.)

On the first day of each new quarter (or the first business day after), you will take a profit distribution. Remember, the Profit Account serves a few purposes:

1. Cash reserves.
2. Metric to measure growth.
3. Profit.

Tally the total amount of profit in the account (don't add any quarterly distributions percentages from deposits you received this day, yet) and take 50% of the money as profit. The other half remains in the account, as a reserve.

No matter what day you start doing Profit First, take a distribution for the current quarter on the first day of the new quarter. For example, let's say you decide to implement Profit First on August 12th. You allocate to your multiple accounts from that day forward. Then, on October 1st, or the first day of the new quarter that you do your bookkeeping, you distribute the profit in the Profit Account. Whether you start this process on July 3rd or September 31st, the next quarter still begins as of October 1st; so you distribute profits for the prior quarter that day. It doesn't matter when you start doing Profit First; what matters is that you get into a quarterly rhythm.

Welcome to the big leagues. You will now take a distribution every quarter, just like large public companies do. They announce their quarterly income and then distribute a portion of the profits to shareholders. And that's exactly what you are going to do (see, you are all grown up now). Quarterly is a great rhythm, by the way. It is a long enough time between distributions that you start looking forward to them, anticipating them. But it isn't so frequent that they come to feel like a normal part of your personal income.

Every quarter, you will take 50% of what is in the account, and leave 50% alone. For example, let's say you have saved $5000 in your Profit Account during the first quarter of implementing Profit First. On the first day of the new quarter, you will take $2500 as a distribution to the equity owners and leave the other 50% intact.

If your company has multiple owners, the distributed profit is divided up based on the percentage owned by each equity owner. Following the above scenario, if you own 60% of the company, another partner owns 35% and an angel investor owns 5%, the distribution would be $1500 (for you, the 60% owner), $875 (for the 35% guy) and $125 (for the investor).

The key is this: The profit distribution may *never* go back to the company. You can't use a fancy term like "plowback" or "profit retention." No term you use will cover up the fact that you are stealing from Paul to pay Peter.

Your business must run on the money it generates for its operating expenses. The plowback of profits means you aren't operating efficiently enough to run on the operating expenses. And if you give the profit back, you won't experience the very important reward of your company serving you. You'll just be letting the monster loose again. So always take your profit, every quarter, and use it for your own purposes. It's celebration time!

CELEBRATION TIME!

When you take your profit distribution, the money is only to be used for one purpose: for your personal benefit. Maybe you go out for a nice dinner with your family. Maybe you get that awesome new couch you have your eye on. Maybe you go on a dream vacation.

In the four years since Jorge and Jose started implementing Profit First in their business, they have taken several dream vacations— Bermuda, Europe, cruises—and have given those vacations to their loved ones as well. These guys know how to celebrate!

"Before we started using Profit First in our business, we were a little bit lost and wondered when the business would take off and improve our lifestyle," Jorge told me. "I don't think anyone wants to work just for the paycheck. You need more incentive. Now, at the end of the quarter, we really look forward to planning what we're going to do with the extra money."

Whatever it is, you *must* use your profits on you! Why? Because this is how you turn Frankenstein, that cash-eating monster, into a cash cow that keeps giving to you and supporting you. Every quarter, with every profit you celebrate, you will fall more and more in love with your business.

PAY UNCLE SAM

Every quarter, you will also pay your quarterly estimated tax. Your accountant probably gave you estimates of how much you owe in taxes; now you pay them. You will reduce some of the pain you feel when paying estimates, because on this very same day each quarter, you also will take that profit for yourself, above and beyond your salary.

ONE SMALL STEP

Each quarter, you need to evaluate your current percentages and move them closer to your TAPs. You can move any percentage you choose to get to your TAPs, but know this—the goal is to never take a step back. I would much rather you take a small step closer to your target Profit Percentage than take a big leap toward it, only to step it back a month later.

If you are adjusting and tweaking your percentages conservatively, I suggest that you account for three percentage points each quarter. That is, you could move your Profit Account from 5% to 8%. Or you could move your Tax Account from 11% to 12%, your Profit Account from 5% to 6% and your Owner's Pay Account from 23% to 24%.

If you can adjust further, go for it, by all means. Just remember, you can't "undo your percentages," because that will undermine this new habit you have established. And don't forget: at the start of next quarter, you will be doing this all over again. Think about what you're doing for a second. You are now distributing profits quarterly, which forces you to find ways to operate more efficiently. Isn't that friggin' cool? Your little company is now doing the same thing as the big kahunas in the industry. While Bloomberg Radio babbles on about "higher than expected" quarterly profits and shareholder distribution by such-and-such public company, you can smile and feel pity for the public stock shareholders and the measly portions they get because *you* own *a lot* of stock in your company. Oh man, does that feel good.

YEAR ONE
FINALIZE YOUR TAXES

Since you're in the quarterly rhythm of evaluating and moving closer to your TAPs, celebrating your profit disbursement and reassessing your expenses, there isn't much of anything special you need to do on a yearly basis. The only thing you need to add to your financial management at year-end is the finalization of your taxes.

Determine how much you owe and how far off you were in your estimates. If you owe more than you have in your tax account, a few things likely went wrong. You probably didn't save a big enough percentage in your tax account, and/or you didn't check in quarterly with your accountant to see how you were doing throughout the year with your tax reserve.

If you owe taxes at year-end and don't have the money in your tax account, this is the one time you can pull from your Profit Account for a reason other than profit distribution. In fact, you have to. You won't go to jail if you don't have profits to distribute to the owners, but you will go to jail if you don't pay your taxes. In this instance, pull the money you have from your Tax Account and your Profit Account to pay the taxes. Then adjust percentages in your Tax Account to ensure you will have enough for the next year.

When you adjust your tax percentage, reduce your profit percentage by that amount. Yes, you are taking a hit on profits, but next quarter you will work on getting those profits up again. The key now is to make sure you are fully prepared for taxes.

If you have too much money left in your Tax Account, congratulations—you can move that money to your Profit Account and take a profit distribution. You may also be able to reduce your Tax TAP and increase your profit allocation percentage by that amount. Just check with your financial expert first.

RAINY DAY FUND

As your profits accumulate in your Profit Account, and you only take half as a profit distribution, the remainder will act as a rainy day fund. You sort of become your own bank. This is a good thing, but too much cash on hand can be a liability (people like to sue deep pockets); and money should be invested, not allowed to sit and stagnate month after month and year after year. This is a simple analysis of what to do with your rainy day fund. First accumulate a three-month cash reserve for your business, so you have enough cash saved to operate unscathed for three months if all sales came to a screeching halt and not another penny came into the business. Then, when you see that the money in your Profit Account is in excess of a three-month reserve, you know this is a good opportunity to put money back into the business, to make some appropriate capital investments that will bring a lot more growth and a lot more profit, or to fund The Vault Account (that's a little teaser for what you will be learning in a little bit).

FOREVER

The Instant Assessment gave you the TAPs, but you can do better. Like an athlete assessing her performance over time, as you use the Profit First system, you will get a good sense of when and where you can push aspects of your business to the next, world-class level. If you can, push for 22% profit, or higher, or cut expenses down to 15%.

Even with you, and all the financial folks who help you in your business, following Profit First, you're still not finished. You can get every single person in your business, regardless of what they do, supporting the business with Profit First. They will do it by implementing a new type of to-do list.

In my second book, *The Pumpkin Plan,* I explain colossal seed-to-business growth—the intersection of uniqueness, top customer demand and systems. Your uniqueness (unique offering) is what makes money, but that only happens when your top customers want your offering. If you can deliver it to them on automatic, you have the potential to become a colossal force in your industry. These three factors form a new, better way to create and maintain a to-do list. You will use three symbols: a $ (dollar sign), a ☺ (smiley face) and an ∞ (infinity symbol).

From today forward, your team can quickly determine their most profitable tasks. If something will likely make money for the company within the next sixty days, give it a $. If it is something for a top client, give it a smiley face ☺; and if it is a system that can be created so that other people or things can do the task perfectly and you no longer need to do it, give it a ∞.

TYPE	PRIORITY	DEFINITION
$ ☺ ∞	1	Create a repeatable system that will make money in the next 60 days by serving a client (e.g. a website design that can be a template for many future clients' sites)
$ ☺	2	Generate revenue in the next 60 days from an existing client (e.g. a sales quote for an existing client)
$ ∞	3	Generate revenue from new clients and result in a repeatable system (e.g. a new product launch)
☺ ∞	4	Cater to clients and result in a repeatable system, but not generate money directly (e.g. implementing project management software)
$	5	Generate revenue within the next 60 days (e.g. a sales quote for a prospect)
☺	6	Serve an existing client, but won't directly result in revenue (e.g. modification to an existing contract at client's request)
∞	7	Create repeatable systems (e.g. form email responses to common questions)
(blank)	8	Though relevant and possibly important, won't generate revenue in the next 60 days, don't serve an existing client and won't create a repeatable system

Figure 6. Task Management List

Next, write down the tasks you have. Code each of them with no symbol (if it doesn't apply to the three categories above), or one of the symbols above. In some cases, a task will get two symbols or all three. Then prioritize your to-do list based upon the symbols in this order:

First do $ ☺ ∞ These are God's gifts to tasks. When you do one of these, you will make money, make a client happy (which, by the way, is the most powerful form of marketing) and systematize the task as a repeatable process. That way, the next time this task presents itself, you just hand it off and it will be done perfectly! Profit with a client loving it, *and* you will be able to do this on automatic going forward.

Next is $ ☺ Happy client paying you money = a happy life.

Then $ ∞ This is a task that lets you make money *and* develop a system to make it happen automatically. Maybe not for the current client, but automatic money usually means new clients down the road.

Then do ☺∞ This is a task that makes a client happy. You will develop a system so that it happens on automatic. Consider it automatic client retention and automatic marketing.

Then do $ This task means you are bringing in money. Profit, baby!

Next, do ☺ You might not make money immediately by performing this task, but a happy client is key to sustainability, is powerful marketing and usually leads to more money in the future.

Then do ∞ With this task, you build a system so that you don't have to do it anew every time.

And lastly, do " " That is a blank. I just put the air quotes there so you could see it was blank. In many cases, as you think of tasks and write them down, you will notice that most are blanks—they don't or won't make money in the near future, they don't serve clients and they aren't building systems. Do these things last.

By having everyone at your company prioritize their to-do lists with this simple system, you push Profit First. Don't just give this to-do system to a few people. Share it with your entire staff. Help them focus on the three things that matter most: profit (the lifeblood of your business, without which you can't sustain the business), clients (the real boss; without them there is no business); and systems (the only way you can grow and compete).

• • •

Jorge and Jose are living the American dream. Just ask them— they'll tell you they are most definitely living the life they set out to experience when they first opened the doors of Specialized ECU Repair. If you follow the steps outlined in this book, you too will look back on your first Profit First year with awe and appreciation. You'll be living the dream, baby!

ACTION STEPS
GET READY FOR A GREAT YEAR

Step 1: Go back to the beginning of the chapter and complete all of the "Day One" tasks outlined there: notify your accountant, set up your accounts (if you haven't done so already), and make your first Profit Account deposit or transfer.

Step 2: Start a "celebration list": come up with ideas for how you to spend your quarterly owner's distribution. Include small treats and big indulgences. Post the list where you can see it, for inspiration and motivation and as a reminder when the quarter comes around and you convince yourself there are more practical uses for the money.

Step 3: Based on the system I shared in this chapter, revamp your to-do list and start using it immediately. You can download blank Profit First To-Do forms at—you guessed it—the Resources tab at MikeMichalowicz.com.

6 DESTROYING DEBT

WELL-DRESSED poverty is still poverty. Just because your business is making lots of money doesn't mean you're hanging onto it. Too many entrepreneurs believe that the top line is what defines success and then behave accordingly. Another big client comes on board, and the entrepreneur expands the office. A big sale rolls in, and with it a fancy dinner. It's like putting Frankenstein's monster in a tuxedo and having it dance and sing to "Puttin' On the Ritz" (shout-out to Mel Brooks). The monster may look as if it has its act together, but it doesn't. One tiny bit of faulty wiring—like, the big client decides not to pay its bills—and the monster goes on a rampage. Everything falls apart.

Two years ago, my cell phone rang with a call from my friend Pete. I was expecting the call—we had plans to have dinner in New York City that weekend and, since Pete is a resident of The Big Apple, he knows all the hot spots. I figured he was calling to confirm plans. The call was not what I expected.

"I'm sorry Mike, I can't do dinner this weekend," Pete said, his voice strained.

"Damn, that sucks. I was really looking forward to it. But no problem, brother. Let's reschedule," I said, looking at my calendar. "What's going on? Heading out of town?"

"Yeah, kinda. Well, not really," Pete replied. Then he sighed and said, "I, uh… I'm broke, Mike. I'm broke."

Pete explained that his bank had called his line. I'm not sure if you're familiar with this experience, but here's how it works: You get a revolving line of credit from the bank. It's a bank account that functions like a credit card, in that you can draw as much money from it as you want, up to your credit limit, and pay it back over time. As long as you pay your interest and make your minimum percentage payment every month, you're good.

Except there's this pesky little rule in the fine print that says the bank can call back the entire loan at any time. Even if you've paid your monthly percentage on time every month, even if you're not carrying a high balance, the bank can yank your line of credit without warning. And once the bank calls to notify you that they're calling your line, the clock starts ticking. You have thirty days to pay back every single penny. Tick. Tick. Tick.

Pete got the call. His line? A million bucks. The amount he had drawn from the line? *A million bucks.* The amount in his company's cash reserves that he could tap into? Zero. Needless to say, dinner in Manhattan was off.

Struggling to get the words out, Pete said, "Mike, can you help me? I'll follow your lead. I'll do anything. If you told me to run naked in the streets, I'd do it."

Of course I agreed to help him find a way to dig himself out of this massive debt. A Lady Godiva-like naked romp through the streets of New York might get him some attention and give me enough razzing fodder for years to come, but it surely wouldn't address his debt (in fact it would probably add to it, what with the fine for lewd and lascivious behavior). So we spent two hours on the phone that night, going over Profit First in detail. At first Pete was confused—why was I talking about profit when he was so far in the hole? You may be feeling this way, too. I get it. It's awfully hard to think about profit, let alone plan for it, when your situation is as dire as Pete's. You may not have a million dollars in debt, but I'll bet that whatever debt you're carrying feels like it might as well be a million dollars, at times.

This is the ultimate survival moment. If you focus all of your energy on paying down debt, that is all you will ever achieve. You'll still be caught in the trap of top line thinking, which will likely result in more debt.

Again, there are similarities here to weight loss. If you're overweight, at a certain point your "credit line" will be called. Maybe you'll see yourself in a family photo and realize you can no longer say it's "just a bit of a muffin top," because that muffin top is dropping down to your knees and tickling your toes. Maybe one day you'll get tired of always being tired. Or maybe it will be something much worse—like a heart attack or diabetes—that finally moves you to say, "Enough is enough."

We can trace almost every major change to a pivotal moment when the pain of staying a certain way is greater than the effort to make awareness of it go away. Call it a tipping point or a turning point, a revelation or a wake-up call; whatever name you give it, the choice is the same. Will you fix the crisis or the root of the problem?

When life "calls the line," we take action. The problem is, most of the time the action we take is a reaction, a narrow, driving focus on the alleviation of immediate pain. We move heaven and earth to bail ourselves out of a jam with little thought of creating permanent change. Why do so many people who have lost weight gain it all back (and then some)? Because as soon as they reach their goal, they revert to old habits. Sure, no one wants to drink a gallon of water and eat grapefruit every morning for the rest of their lives, or spend so much time with the Thighmaster that they're going to have to think about going steady with it. The pain of being fat is gone—what's the point of taking another Richard Simmon's Cruise to Lose?

Once the pain is gone, the action we decided to take in that pivotal moment falls away. No more grapefruit. No more water. No more Thighmaster. Grapefruit is replaced with grape jellybeans. Water turns to soda. And the Thighmaster is tossed into the basement where all good intentions go to die. Is it any wonder that when the weight comes back, it's with a vengeance? After all, your mind now knows you can lose weight in a pinch. Who cares if you gain a few pounds? You can always crash diet again, right? Try out for *The Biggest Loser*? And of course there's always "the surgery."

What my friend Pete intended to do was the same deal, different crisis. He had had the equivalent of a financial heart attack. As soon as his big moment hit, he became a man on a mission—crush that debt immediately! By whatever means necessary, he would dig himself out of the crisis. His actions (or reactions) were the equivalent of a crash diet. He wasn't giving any thought to how to make his business *permanently* healthy.

If Pete manages to survive this crisis in crash diet mode, what are the chances he will find himself in a similar situation—or worse—a few months or years from now? The chances are high—so high I would say it's a sure bet.

Even when you and your business are in debt up to your eyeballs, you must establish a habit of putting your profit first. You must still (and always) pay yourself first. When you get into the habit of fiscal health based on this system, you will fix the problem permanently. Financial crises will be a thing of the past, because if someone calls your line, you'll have the cash to cover it.

Here is what I told Pete: "If you have debt, be it one thousand, one million or somewhere in between, you need to kill that debt once and for all while still slowly and methodically building profit."

The Profit First system I'm teaching you will keep your focus on a super-healthy business, working in your sweet spot to produce goods and provide services for ideal clients. This laser focus will automatically keep your costs down, allowing you to pay off debt faster and eventually increase your Profit Percentage. The tweak is, when you distribute profits, ninety-nine percent of the money goes to paying down debt. The remaining one percent goes toward rewarding yourself. This way, the debt gets hit just as aggressively, but you still strengthen your Profit First habit.

In short, if you wait to implement Profit First until after you pay down your debt, you are less likely to ever build the business efficiencies that will permanently eradicate your debt and create a perpetual profit stream. Start the habit now, and eventually that ninety-nine percent will go toward building up your cash reserves and your own owner distribution.

ANOTHER SIMPLE SOLUTION MOST PEOPLE DON'T BELIEVE ACTUALLY WORKS

By now I hope you're a member of the "How healthy is your business?" club. Are you wearing the t-shirt? I am. What? Don't have one? Don't know where to get your own? I'll give you a hint—it's in your closet. Sharpie, old t-shirt, "Profit First" on the front, "How healthy is your business?" on the back. Ten seconds. Done. What? Did you think I was going to give you a link to my online store? Hardly. A profitable business happens when you save your pennies at every turn, my friend. That's how we club members roll. Frugal. Not cheap, but frugal, for sure. And that is how I ended up with the homemade masterpiece I'm currently sporting—and a healthy cash reserve that is about to send my family and me on a nice vacation, where I will wear my awesome t-shirt with pride, thank you very much!

Getting that healthy business all boils down to one really, really simple formula: You must consistently spend less money than you make.

Duh, right? I'm sure you knew that. Everyone knows that. So why do so few people follow it? Spending less than you make every day, every week, every month, every year, every decade leads to wealth and freedom from financial stress. And yet most of us can't seem to do this one simple thing.

Here again we're talking logic versus human behavior. If logic worked for us humans, we'd all be rich. I wouldn't be writing this book to tell you how to do this, because you would already be doing it. Instead, I would have one of my minions swim from my big yacht over to your even bigger yacht to ask if you could spare some Grey Poupon. Then we would both chuckle at the complete absurdity of the situation. I mean, who would have the audacity to eat anything with a common man's mustard like Grey Poupon?

This is the challenge all of humanity faces: We know what we have to do, but we still don't do it. Why is that? Why do so many of us consistently fail to become rich and accumulate debt instead? Why? *Why*? (Picture me on my knees, dramatically banging my fist on the ground and shouting, "Why, why?" like Scarlett O'Hara in *Gone with the Wind*.)

Fortunately for us, Suze Orman has the answer.

Now, let me say something about Ms. Orman. I am a *huge* fan. However, I have never watched her show on CNN and, aside from one book (which I still haven't read in its entirety), I have not purchased any of her products. I'm a fan of hers because I saw a lecture she gave on PBS one Sunday morning.

I like to write early on Sunday mornings, when all is quiet in the house. But on this particular morning I decided to brew a pot of coffee and channel surf instead. Thank God I did. As I flipped through the channels, I saw Suze Orman talking to a group of about fifty people. I had heard of her and seen her picture a million times, and I was curious to see how she presented in a public speaking format. Maybe I could glean some tips and tricks on being a better presenter. And let me tell you, she is really good. I have seen hundreds of speakers, and she truly impressed the heck out of me.

While explaining personal financial strategy to the audience she stopped, looked around the room and said, "The solution to debt is this simple: If you want to get out of debt, you must get more enjoyment out of saving your money than you do spending your money."

This was a life-changing realization for me. I put down my coffee and stared out the window. Suze continued to speak, but I was so caught up in my a-ha moment, I heard nothing. I just kept repeating what she said about saving versus spending over and over in my head. "That's it," I thought. Wealth is a game of emotion. Business success is a game of emotion. Profit First is a game of emotion. It all comes down to the story we tell ourselves about what we're doing. "Is what I'm doing making me happy, or not?"

When something makes you happy in the moment, you'll keep doing it. If spending makes you happy, you'll spend more. Period. And that spending can be on anything from a new tie to a new hire to new mountains of debt. If saving makes you happy, you'll look for any opportunity to save more. Coupons, sales, bargain bins—heaven. Saving one hundred percent because you eliminated the expense entirely? *Nirvana*.

Listening to Suze that day, the whole "pain and pleasure" motivation that Anthony Robbins has talked about for years finally made sense to me. The pain moment is the kick in the ass, when you finally say enough is enough. Pain gives you a big shove out the door. For me, the pain moment was my daughter sliding her piggy bank toward me, trying to save our family from absolute financial ruin. For Pete, it was a call from the bank.

But pain just gets you to take enough action to get out of immediate pain. Then it stops working. Suze was teaching me the other half: pleasure. (Don't do it. Don't let your mind go there. And… there it went. Keep reading when you get your mind out of the gutter, pervert. I'll wait.)

The premise is simple—we avoid pain and move toward pleasure, putting a significant emphasis on the moment (remember the Recency Effect) and very little emphasis on the long term. Immediate pain gets the ball rolling, but pleasure keeps it moving. You probably picked up this book because of pain, and you will likely see results quickly because your efforts will reduce the pain. But the only way you will be able to make this work forever is if you get immediate pleasure each time you exercise your new habits. Just as at the gym, you can only work out so many times before the pain of seeing your muffin top in the mirror isn't worth all the effort anymore… and it is at that exact moment that you most need to derive true joy from working out, because it is what will help keep you fit and trim forever.

If you are stuck in the grow-more/spend-more mode and accumulating debt, it isn't because you don't understand the numbers. You are absolutely *not* an idiot. The problem is assuredly linked to your emotions. You are getting instant—albeit momentary—pain relief, because your mind believes that your investment will bring results (the hope of future and permanent returns). When this doesn't happen, you slip back into panic, sell like a mad dog and spend (more often using the friendly term "invest") to grow. You find momentary pain relief in making some type of progress. But when it fails to yield more cash in your pocket, the pain comes back. It's a nasty cycle.

Fortunately, the fix is simple, if you allow it to be: Give yourself more joy when you choose *not* to spend money than you do when you choose to spend it. Give yourself more joy when your bottom line grows (not just the top line). Give yourself tons of joy when your Profit Percentage grows.

You do this by acknowledging it to yourself. I don't care if you feel like Stuart Smalley giving yourself a pep talk in the mirror; you must train your mind to find joy in implementing the Profit First system. (One of the best ways to find joy in this is to hang out with other Profit First entrepreneurs. Everything is more fun when you share the experience with others. I'll talk more about this in Chapter 8, when I teach you how to participate in an accountability group—a Profit Accelerator Group or Profit Pod.)

When you opt not to spend money, acknowledge it. Give yourself a pat on the back. Do a happy dance. Celebrate every time you save— whether it's ten bucks or ten thousand. Put on your favorite music and crank it, get really happy. Embarrass your kids at the mall. Heck, embarrass yourself. Don your new Profit First Sharpie t-shirt, sans trousers, and post that one on Facebook. Over time you will train your mind to equate happiness and celebration with choosing saving money over spending it (and perhaps walking around malls in a t-shirt and tighty-whities).

It's hard to get by without food or water, and toilet paper is a really handy thing to have. When you do have to spend money, reward yourself for getting the best deal possible. Find a good price for the essential things you need and don't buy the nonessentials. Then start the t-shirt celebration all over again.

THE "JUST ONE MORE DAY" GAME

Remember the story about how I lost my first fortune by becoming the Angel of Death? You might remember that, in the end, all but one of the companies I invested in went belly up. The lone survivor was Hedgehog Leatherworks. The owner, Paul Scheiter, is an amazing guy. I consider him my best friend. I shared some of the success strategies we employ at Hedgehog in *The Toilet Paper Entrepreneur* and *The Pumpkin Plan,* so if you read those books then Paul probably seems like your best friend, too.

Recently I went to visit Paul at his place in St. Louis, Missouri. As we drove by a Home Depot on the way to his leather shop, he said, "Oh, I need to get some electrical stuff for the office."

Then he smiled and kept driving.

"Why don't we pick it up?" I asked.

"I will," he replied. "In just one more day."

The next day we drove by the same Home Depot. Paul looked at the sign, grinned from ear to ear, then looked away and drove on.

I said, "Don't we need the electrical supplies?"

"Absolutely we do. Just one more day."

This pattern went on for the entire week. At the end of my visit, Paul drove me to the airport. Just before we pulled up to my drop-off point, I asked him why he hadn't yet bought the electrical supplies he needed. That's when he shared his "Just One More Day" technique. I had some time before my flight, so we pulled over to short-term parking. During the next half hour, he laid it all out for me.

Paul understands the formula, spend less + make more = wealth. He also understands that for this formula to work, both factors in the equation must provide him with an emotional win.

It's easy to feel happy about making more money, but to achieve real wealth you also have to train yourself to feel happy when you spend less. Paul achieves this by rewriting the formula in his mind. His version is (+spend less) + (+make more) = wealth. In Paul's formula both spending less and making more are positives. Not surprisingly, his formula is like the Profit First Formula; it prioritizes human behavior, not logic.

When Paul needs to purchase something, he plays the "Just One More Day" game. He challenges himself to go just one more day without the item. Every time he passes up an opportunity to buy whatever he needs, he gets pumped. He gets a high from going without for one more day. Sometimes, while playing this game, Paul discovers that he no longer needs the product or service he intended to buy. Playing the game opens up other possibilities, and truly tests how badly you need something. Sometimes you can't get around it—you have to spend money on something because you actually need it. But by waiting "just one more day," you are not only keeping operating cash in your account for one more day; you are giving yourself another day to come up with alternatives.

THE WORST MONTH

If you're like most entrepreneurs, your personal income is wildly unpredictable. It changes month by month, depending on sales and collections. We're a hopeful bunch, entrepreneurs—we have to have the nerve to launch a business in the first place. So it's no surprise that most entrepreneurs are bamboozled by their hopes and look at their best revenue months as the new normal, when very often it is not. Until your best month becomes your average month, it's not the norm; it's the exception.

When you base decisions on your best revenue month, you will run out of cash—quickly. Debt will start to pile up. And you will go back to your old standby, "sell more—grow, grow, grow!" Acting as if your best month is the norm is one surefire way to keep yourself locked in the Survival Trap.

In fact, accountants joke about this. I had a call with Andrew Hill and Gary Nunn, the founders of Solutions Tax & Bookkeeping in Frisco, Texas, about the spending habits of entrepreneurs, and they told me the inside joke. Whenever a client approaches them about a windfall of new money, the client will inevitably say, "I don't even know how I would ever spend all this money."

Each time, Andrew and Gary have the same response: "Oh, you'll find a way. And you'll probably figure it out within the next month."

Maybe that insiders' joke isn't ROTFLMAO (Rolling On The Floor, Laughing My Ass Off) funny to you, but it is to Andrew and Gary. They hear the same comments from entrepreneurs all the time, and in every case, by the next month, the money is gone. Every. Time.

That's why percentages are such a valuable tool. As an entrepreneur, your income varies. Some months are great; some months suck; and most are average. But it is typical behavior for entrepreneurs to look at their best month and tell themselves, "This is my new normal"—and then start spending and taking from the business accordingly.

Percentages are based on real results—the cash in the bank. No games, no hypotheticals, no, "We'll make it up next month." Projections are an opinion. Cash is a fact.

The percentages put a varying sum of money into your different accounts, such as Owner's Pay, every 10th and 25th; and then you draw your owner's salary from that account based on the pay you allotted. If you have more money in the account then you take in salary, the difference in money stays and accumulates. This way, when (notice I didn't say if) a slow month happens, money has accumulated in your Owner's Pay Account and your salary stays consistent. If the money in the Owner's Pay Account is not enough to pay your salary, you can't take it. You need to make a hard decision about cutting other costs, and you'd better kick ass growing the top line with great clients, too.

So how do you predict the owner's salary your company will likely support? Look at your slowest three months and average them. That is the lowest your revenue will likely ever go. Then determine the percentage of this income that will be allocated to Owner's Pay (35% for example, times the average monthly revenue for the three worst months). Every quarter, we will do a salary raise based on how much money is in the Owner's Pay Account and whether it is accumulating faster than we are withdrawing it. Take the bump that you can reasonably take based upon your twelve-month, rolling average. As long as the account accumulates more cash or stays even, you are taking a healthy salary (one that your company can healthily support).

THE DEBT FREEZE

I've taught you how to ensure your business is profitable immediately—from your very next deposit. Now I'm going to teach you how to immediately stop accumulating debt, and to destroy the debt you currently have. I call the method you are about to learn the "Debt Freeze." It will guide your business through a rapid pay-down of accumulated debt and a freeze of new debt, both while continuing your Profit First habit.

Now, don't panic. I'm not asking you to sell everything and move into a van down by the river. I'm not even asking you to stop spending entirely. That can irreparably damage your business. I am simply asking you to commit to a spending freeze that will free you from debilitating debt. The goal here is to cut cost, not to compromise the business. You can fire all your people, shut down your website, refuse to pay a penny to anyone and seriously move into a van down by the river with your new roommate and struggling motivational speaker, Matt Foley. . . but you'll be out of business. You want to cut out the fat of your business, the stuff that is not generating or supporting income for your company. But you don't want to cut out the muscle, the stuff that you absolutely must have to deliver your product or service.

You need to know where you stand. The first step is to assess where you are today. Fear is only amplified by a lack of knowledge. If you don't know your exact numbers, your mind goes wild and says crazy things (like. . . "Ahh. . . I am going broke. . . ahh. . . the only thing worse is Mike dressed up like Scarlett O'Hara. Ahh. . . what the hell am I thinking? Ahh!"). You can't change what you don't acknowledge, so you need to know exactly what you're dealing with. And when you know what you are dealing with, your mind doesn't drift nearly as much.

For those of us who get happy when we save (remember Suze's speech?), the Debt Freeze is a rave party. To be clear, this is my kind of party, and I'm a freak. When you see the crazy debt-reduction fun we have planned, you might want to back out the front door as quickly as possible. But, if you want to be debt free forever, stick around. Here are the steps to getting your party started:

PRINT AND MARKUP DOCS

1. Print out your current income statement for the last twelve months, as well as your current accounts payable report, your credit card statements, loan statements and any other statements related to debt, and your last twelve months of payments made from any of your business bank accounts. If you do not have an income statement ready, just gather the other documents.

2. With a highlighter, draw a box around any labor costs— salaries, commissions and bonuses for employees.

Exclude owner salaries and payments to freelancers and subcontractors.

3. Now highlight expenses that were required to generate immediate revenue. For example, if you are a private investigator, you might highlight the purchase of a USB drive you use to store evidence that you give to your clients. If you bought a USB drive that you do *not* give to clients and just use internally, that item would not be highlighted.

4. Next, highlight any expenses that are absolutely necessary to keep your business open. This does not include employees or contractors, or any people you boxed with your highlighter already in Step 3. If you have a spy car that is outfitted for surveillance and you need it to—well, spy—highlight it. If you have a spy car that really isn't a spy car, it's just your ride, don't highlight it.

5. With a red pen, circle expenses that repeat every month, quarter or year and will continue to do so. Note: Some expense items, like labor costs, will get highlighted or boxed *and* circled.

NOW LET'S DO SOME MATH

6. Add up all the expenses for the year; include everything you highlighted, circled, boxed or left blank. Exclude tax payments and owner's distributions or salaries. Divide the result by twelve to determine your monthly "nut"—the total amount you have decided you need to cover each month.

7. Determine the difference between your current monthly operating expenses and the number it *must* be according to your Instant Assessment. For example, if you currently have $52,000 in average monthly expenses and your Instant Assessment has your monthly expenses at $30,000, you need

to cut your operating expenses by $22,000. Period. There will be no justifying past spending mistakes, no saying, "But I need everything." You don't. Your healthy, booming competitor has figured it out. You need to put on your big-girl panties and accept that you spent too much, and today is the day we fix it. (Kinda creepy that I know you wear big-girl panties, isn't it?)

8. Band-Aids come off more easily when you tear them off. Chipping away a little debt here and a little debt there prolongs the agony; rarely fixes a company fast enough; never changes your behaviors to those that truly put profit first; and is really, really scary for your employees. Cutting back a few things (or people) at a time puts your employees (and you) in a constant state of uncertainty. Ripping off the Band-Aid will make you scream in pain momentarily, but the healing starts right away. The same is true with debt.

   To avoid having to keep chipping away at debt, it's best to plan to cut expenses until you are operating at 10% *below* the target number on your Instant Assessment. So if we know we need to cut expenses down to $30,000 to be in the Profit First range for operating expenses, we want to do what we can to cut down to $27,000 (that extra 10%). Why? Because when you cut expenses, you may realize that something has a negative effect on your business, and you can't replace it with a timely alternative. You may need to take a few expenses back on. I call this "expense bounce-back." It happens—we just need to prepare for it.

BUILD A LEANER TEAM

9. Labor cost is usually the most expensive part of operating any business. This is the first expense you put a highlighted box around on your income statement, and you almost definitely circled it in red pen, too. If your company is

racking up debt, it is all too often because labor cost is too high. The problem with cutting labor cost is, our minds quickly defend and justify why people should stay: "I own the company;" "I can't do the work;" "I need to direct my team to do the work." Plus, they need a job (which is true), they are integral to the company (probably also true), the company will tank without them (super unlikely), and if I get rid of them I won't have people to do the work (hardly ever true).

Overstaffed entrepreneurs have either tried to get themselves out of doing work as quickly as possible (they like to think they are managers now, or better yet, they need to spend extraordinary amounts of time on the corporate "vision") or believe that systems aren't core to a business (which they are). You need to let go of people. And you have got to realize that switching from working *in* the business to *on* the business is not like flipping a light switch. It is gradual. Often, the most under-used employee in an overstaffed company is you, the owner. It's time you get back to actually doing the work, and in the future we will slowly transition you from *in* to *on*.

Now, back to your overstaffed company. Evaluate each person and determine if her role is mandatory for operations to continue (not the person, but the role). If a person wears multiple hats (for example is your receptionist and in-house sales person), ask yourself if each role is mandatory for operations to continue.

10. Next, evaluate your staff. Are there any people who aren't "A-players"? Do you have any people who are actually bad for the company? Those people are costing you money in more ways than one.

11. Ignoring the salaries and how you feel about the people, determine the following: a) which roles must stay in-house

no matter what, b) which roles could be outsourced and c) which roles the company can continue without.

12. Next, look at your people. Look at yourself. What roles could you take on? Now look at your best employees, the A-players. Can they be shifted around to cover the roles that must stay in-house? Are there any must-have roles that can only be handled by a specific person?

13. Plan the layoffs. Now, before I get into this, I want you to know that I know how devastating it is. I know how much you will want to resist ever doing this, because I did. There was a day when I had to lay off ten people out of my twenty-five-employee company. It was the most difficult day of my professional life. I had to lay off nearly half my staff, not because they did anything wrong, but because *I did*—I mismanaged the numbers; I hired quickly and often and unnecessarily.

I also want you to know that no matter how devastating it is, laying people off is necessary. Trying to keep a few employees your company cannot afford will only put your company under, thereby ensuring that *everyone* loses their job. And, because you prioritize the layoff of poorly-performing staff and people who fill roles that are not a core need for your company, you are not just saving the cost of keeping these people on; you are also building a more efficient infrastructure.

Keep in mind that in letting these people go, you are freeing them to find a job that is a better fit. Yes, it sucks that you need to fire the people you hired on good faith. But it would be worse if you kept them in a dead-end job. I know this firsthand. Just this morning I looked up the LinkedIn profiles of the ten people I had to lay off that terrible day. All of them have better jobs. Three are managing partners at significant industry firms; another is living her lifelong dream of sailing around the world; one is a now a judge; one is a stay-at-home mom (which, my wife likes to remind me, *is* the ultimate job)! None of this would have happened if they had stayed at my unprofitable little company.

14. Call your employment and/or business attorney. (For a list of lawyers who are also PFPs, go to MikeMichalowicz. com and check out the Resources section.) These attorneys understand the law, will review your employment agreements and make sure you handle your layoffs properly. Never, and I mean never, proceed with terminations or layoffs without talking with your attorney first.

15. Among the highlighted, boxed expenses, you also have commissions and bonuses for employees, freelancers, etc. Look for ways to cut down on or remove these costs entirely, but always remember that in doing so, you are reducing someone's pay. Staff or freelancers handed a notice of reduction in income are likely become disgruntled or disheartened; no matter how you deal with it, expect the news to kill morale and weaken productivity.

16. Start the layoffs. Choose a second person (perhaps your business partner, or your HR director, or, if you don't have anyone in-house, bring in your attorney—this is one of the few costs you do want to incur) to witness the layoffs and help you explain the situation with each employee. Meet with each person. With the approval of your attorney, first explain the reason for the layoff to your employee and then provide support that you can afford, like circulating his résumé or even paying some severance.

17. Once each person is laid off, call a staff meeting with all your remaining employees. Share what you have done and why you did it. Explain how difficult it is to have to do

this, and that you take responsibility for both the financial problem you got the company into and for fixing it. Assure your team that everyone remaining is here to stay, and that you have taken action to immediately stabilize the company.

Do not, I repeat do not, ask people to take a pay cut. I did this with dire consequences. Asking all your people to continue to work just as hard or harder than ever for less money is worse for the emotional welfare of your company than letting just one more person go. When I did this, it disheartened the entire team. I was simultaneously telling them to step up for the company and cover their own work as well as that of the people who had left and that, as a reward for their efforts, I would cut their salary by 10%! They felt disheartened and fearful that the cuts would continue. Of the people remaining, nearly half of them started looking for a new job with a more stable company. All of a sudden there were a lot of sick days, and one of my key remaining guys decided not to remain. He got a job elsewhere.

TIME FOR MORE CUTS

18. Now the hardest part is over, call your bank and tell them to stop all automatic withdrawals from all of your accounts, except for any that you have highlighted in Steps 2 and 3. Then notify your vendors that you are stopping the withdrawals and will pay by check going forward. I am not suggesting in any way that you should not pay what you owe, or break a commitment. I simply want you to be acutely aware of every payment you make.

19. Call each credit card company for which you have a card and ask them to issue you a new card with a new number. Tell the credit card company that no payments that were being processed on your old card should transfer to your new one. (Many credit card companies do this for you as

a convenience, and this is a convenience that you do not want.) You need to do this because your cards have been compromised—by you. This step will stop all automatic charges. Then, just as you did in the previous step, notify each vendor that you are putting a halt to the automatic charges.

Those recurring fees can be insidious. I got trapped in a recurring gym membership fee. I would see it on my credit card, and since it was "only $29" a month, I let it go. I wasn't going to the gym anymore, but I told myself, "I should go to the gym. I'll keep the charge because I'll use it at some time this month."

Then one day my credit card was replaced because of suspicious activity. (I wondered if my credit card company was suspicious about how I could be a gym member for so long *and* a regular McDonald's customer). The day the card was canceled, the gym membership payment stopped. I had forgotten about the gym membership entirely, and didn't even notice the charge on my monthly bill. When the gym called to get a replacement card, I canceled the membership. I got curious about how long I had been auto-paying the gym. Turned out I had only gone a total of six times over nearly seventeen months, which breaks down to six hours of use for just under $500.

But the story doesn't end here. This is when I realized I wasn't working out nearly enough, so I called some friends and started exercising with them. One of them has a membership to the same gym and can bring a guest for free once a week. Guess who goes with him? I am averaging fifty-plus workouts per year at the same gym now, at no cost. And he is working out more, too, because he has a motivated workout partner.

The point is this: Cutting costs is something that is very easy to put off for another day. It's the *mañana* syndrome—I'll get to it tomorrow. And for me (and you too, I suspect) those days of putting things off pile up to a year or more very quickly. You will be unable to put off cutting costs anymore simply by getting your credit cards reissued.

20. Cut every single circled red expense that you can. Recurring bills are sneaky; they seem small and insignificant until you look at how much you spend cumulatively, over time. To make this even clearer, multiply a monthly recurring bill by twelve. That is what you are really spending. Put a big "X" through each circled expense you cancel. If you absolutely can't get rid of a circled expense, highlight it on the paper.

21. Renegotiate the highlighted expenses. Everything is up for negotiation—your rent, your credit card rates and debt, your vendors' bills, your software license, your Internet bill, your weight, your height, your age, everything. Your job now is to contact every vendor and get your costs reduced in the most significant way possible without hurting the relationship. Your vendors will not typically be happy with the suggestion of a 50% reduction, so I suggest you start by asking for a 25% reduction in the hope of getting a 10% to 15% savings. But don't just call, do some research first. Find alternative, less expensive providers and be prepared to go to the alternatives.

    Start by negotiating the small, necessary expenses. You want to build your negotiation muscle. Build your way up to the bigger expenses. Negotiation is a whole topic of its own, but for now, realize that being a hard-ass isn't always the most effective approach. Being informed, firm and willing to concede so both sides win is the best method. The goal is to get the same results at a lower cost. It doesn't mean that you need to stick with what you have and get it more cheaply; you can also find alternatives—a different thing, more cheaply. For example, some hotels charge for Internet access in the room and others don't. If you can't get a hotel to remove or reduce the in-room Internet charge, get the lobby password and work there.

22. Put a big check mark next to each highlighted expense you successfully negotiate or replace.

23. Now go through all those expenses that are left on the list. You know, those that you left blank. It's time to wipe them out. Put a big X through each expense that you commit to not incurring again—at least not for another two years. You are going to take a sabbatical from these expenses and discover how much your business can accomplish without unnecessary expenses.

Job done. And if you made it to your target expense reduction without going on a bender, I say job *well* done. Breathe for a few moments. Feel the stress of overwhelming expenses leaving you. This was a hard day, but by completing it you have staged yourself for major profits. Now you're ready to grow your business in an efficient way.

Cutting costs is embarrassing. You have a reputation. You always pay for dinner, or you drive the nice car. You are the "nice" boss who throws pizza parties and gives sweet holiday bonuses. Let me assure you, the relief you feel once you complete the Debt Freeze is way more powerful than the embarrassment you fear.

No matter how much debt you have, know that there is a way out. More than that, know that you are not the first person to be here. Many people have recovered from dire financial situations and the key to doing that is in your hands.

We are on a mission to change the perspective of successful business from "make a lot" to "save a lot." The new definition of success is not about the most revenue, employees and office space but the most profit, generated through the fewest employees and with the least-expensive office space. Make the game one you win based upon efficiency, frugality and innovation, not on size, flair and looks.

IF YOU OWE A BANK A MILLION DOLLARS

There is a saying in the banking industry: "If you owe a bank a thousand dollars, it's your problem. If you owe the bank a million dollars, it's their problem." Remember Pete? After our call, he started a Profit Account, cut expenses like mad and then called the bank. Almost everything is negotiable, and when you owe a bank a million bucks and don't have it, they'll listen to your ideas. Pete worked out a very doable payment plan, and within three months had already whacked out 5% of the debt and turned a profit. And, he joined an accountability group. Mine. We have been keeping each other in check for over two years now, and while I am vowed to confidentiality about Pete's progress, let me just say this... it's been massive. Pete was, understandably, a quivering wreck when he called me that night two years ago. Today he is the epitome of confidence. And Pete did it by implementing the power of small actions, a series of consistent small steps bringing about big results.

LEAST EFFORT, BIGGEST RESULTS

You too must utilize the power of small actions. What is the biggest bang for the buck with the least effort? When it comes to fixing things, we need to build emotional momentum. Kinda like going to the gym. If you go back to the gym for the first time in ten years and work out like a mad dog, you may feel great that first day; but within a day or two, you will be so sore and in so much pain, you will likely never go to the gym again. Momentum rarely occurs after one crazy effort. Momentum builds slowly but relentlessly. Small, repetitive, continuous actions, chained together, build momentous momentum (say that one ten times fast).

In his extraordinary book, *The Total Money Makeover*, Dave Ramsey explains the "Debt Snowball." It's contrary to logic, but plays exactly into the psyche of all of us human beings. Ramsey tells us that logic would say to pay off our debts with the highest interest rates first, but that doesn't build emotional momentum. It is getting to tear up a statement—any statement, because it is fully paid off—that gives you a sense of momentum and gets you charged up to tackle the next one. Ramsey explains that you should sort all your debts from smallest to biggest, regardless of interest rates. Only when two debts are a similar amount should the one with the highest interest rate be paid first.

Ramsey tells us to pay only the minimum on all the debts, except the one at the top of the list—the smallest one. Then put all your financial power into crushing that first debt as fast as possible. Once that first debt is wiped out, then tackle the next one on the list by adding to the minimum payment with the money you were using to pay the first debt. Once the second debt is paid off, go for the next, adding all the money being used to pay the second debt to the minimum of the third. See how the snowball grows? And see how your enthusiasm and excitement about eradicating debt grows? You will get more and more pleasure from not spending than you once did from spending. Suze and Dave would both be so proud of you.

But the trick to Ramsey's method, and Suze's, and mine (and anyone with one iota of sanity) is this: You cannot add new debt as you pay off old. That is just shifting money around, paying down one debt while building another. You need to get your Debt Freeze on. And then destroy debt, once and for all.

ACTION STEPS
DOWN WITH DEBT

Step 1: Start the Debt Freeze. Stop any recurring payments and kill off anything you don't need. Do whatever it takes to get your "monthly nut" down to 10% lower than your Instant Assessment suggests it should be.

Step 2: Start the Debt Snowball. Pay off your smallest outstanding debt first. As you wipe out each bill with recurring payments, use the freed-up money to tackle the next smallest debt.

Bonus: Join the "How healthy is your business?" club. Make your Profit First t-shirt and then post a selfie of you wearing that shirt on Facebook, Twitter or Google+. Be sure to tag me when you do it.

7 FOUND MONEY

I HAVE yet to meet an entrepreneur who hasn't wanted to hire a "rainmaker"—that magical salesperson who, like the companies that say they can give you access to your great-grandmother Sally's unclaimed fortune, will save the day by bringing in big sale after big sale. Never mind the fact that we, the owners and leaders who love our companies and what we do, are the ultimate rainmakers; it is this top line approach to solving a cash flow crisis that holds companies back. Cranking up the sales team in order to "make it rain" is not going to help your company if you don't have efficiencies in place, because ultimately, whatever new client revenue you generate will have corresponding costs. And these are likely to go unchecked.

If you want to increase profitability (and you'd better friggin' want to do that), you must first build efficiencies. Focusing solely on increasing sales is like setting up a bunch of rain barrels next to your house and doing some frantic rain dance in a loincloth while ignoring a massive water source right beneath your feet.

Take Idaho, for example. Ninety-five percent of the state's water supply comes from underground. The 135 mile-long Big Lost River collects water from the Rocky Mountains as it winds through Idaho and then just "disappears" as it goes subterranean. The water from Big Lost River, Snake River and other underground water sources collects in the Snake River Aquifer, which measures 400 miles wide. That is enough water to serve the majority of Idaho's agricultural needs. So that Idaho spud you're munching on is thanks to an underground water supply—not some rain dance Idahoans learned on the Internet (albeit, Idahoans know how to get their funk on), or a band of merry farmers capturing rain in buckets and turned-over cowboy hats.

Why should you care about Idaho and its underground lakes? Because 95% of your company's profitability is contingent on what goes on beneath the surface (after the sales), not what happens in the sky (the sales themselves). And it is what's going on "underground" that will help you "find" gobs of money.

WHY EVEN FAT CATS NEED EFFICIENCY

Recently, I was asked to keynote the Global Student Entrepreneur Awards in Washington, DC, where leading collegiate entrepreneurs from all over the world gather and are recognized for their incredible impact. At breakfast on the morning of the event, I ended up sitting next to Greg Crabtree. Greg is the author of *Simple Numbers, Straight Talk, Big Profits*. Greg caught my attention immediately, talking with another gentleman at our table about college football. I inserted myself into their discussion ("Go Hokies!"), and soon enough the conversation drifted from how this team is better than that one to entrepreneurs and profitability. I remember thinking: "Hold on—we are talking about college football and profitability. There is a God!"

After Greg recounted some information he shares in his book about how to maximize profitability, I asked, "Is there such a thing as too much profit? Is there a ceiling?"

"You always want to expand profit," Greg replied. "In fact, you must, because there are outside forces that will continually take your profitability away—your competition. As you find ways to increase profitability, or even if you don't, your competition is doing the same. Everyone is trying to become more profitable. And as businesses become more profitable, the competitive pressure sets in and prices drop to attract more customers.

"When you figure out a big leap in profitability, the competition will sniff it out, and it is just a matter of time before they do the same thing. Then someone drops prices to get more clients, and everyone else, including you, has to do the same to stay in business. This is how profits get squeezed."

We've seen the phenomena Greg outlined over and over. Consider flat-panel televisions, for example. They became commercially popular in the early 2000s but were still a luxury item until around 2005, when the cost of big screen TVs started dropping 25% each year. By the end of the decade, vendors had dropped the prices so significantly that it seemed retailers were practically giving them away. Then, because manufacturing televisions got easier and easier, profits jumped, but only for a short time. It wasn't long before everyone started dropping prices again to capture demand, to the point where it now seems as though a retailer needs to pay you to take a small or last year's flat-panel model. James Li, the chief executive of Syntax Groups—maker of the Olevia brand of flat-panel televisions—said of his competitors, "If they go to $3000, I will go to $2999."

Another recent example of the profit squeeze phenomenon is the influx of Internet marketers. In early 2000, a few guys figured out that you could make a crappy information product, promote it with a grainy video made in your wood-paneled kitchen, email people with a "last chance to purchase" offer and make a killing. The costs were next to nothing—a webcam, a couple PDF files, an email marketing system and really, really bad lighting—and the returns were huge. Profits approached nearly 100%, but only for a short time.

I suspect the early, "Wild West" years of information marketing were amazing for those entrepreneurs, but within five years the landscape changed. Because the industry was known for achieving high sales and record profits, the competition came in strong. First there was the flood of GRiQs (Get-Rich-Quickers—the folks who pursue fast, easy money and give up just as quickly when they find their scheme requires work). Supply quickly started to outstrip demand, and consumers started requiring higher and higher quality. More sophisticated marketers started making higher and higher quality stuff, which in turn pushed prices down for everyone. That crappy, grainy video and PDF that sold for $1997 (supposedly there is something magical about a seven at the end of a number) in 2000 now sells for a $1.97 and comes with five years of one-on-one coaching in the seller's wood-paneled office. . . ahem, kitchen. Just as in the flat-panel TV business or in any other business, it's "hard" to become profitable in information marketing. And that's how it always goes.

Profit is a slippery animal. When profit margins are big, usually in excess of 20%, people sniff out and almost immediately start to duplicate what you're doing, and look for ways to do it better, faster, and above all, *cheaper* than your company. I'm not, in any way, saying that you should stop investing in efficiency and thereby (temporarily) increase profit. I'm saying that even if you think you're good with profit, you're not. The competition will squeeze you eventually, and soon, so keep finding ways to do what you do better, faster and cheaper.

DO THIS FIRST

By now you've figured out that focusing solely on top line thinking (sales, sales, sales!) does not lead to profitability. In fact more sales, without efficiency, lead to further inefficiency. In other words, more sales make you less profitable. It's a vicious cycle. So before you can focus on sales, you must first nail Efficiency 101—and then take a few advanced classes.

Efficiency increases your profit margins, or, the amount of money you earn as profit on each product or service you offer. It's basic logic, easier than a freshman math class—increased profit margins will boost your company's profits without the need for increased sales. And when you do kick the selling machine into gear (which we will discuss in a few), profits will skyrocket. So the method is simple—achieve greater efficiency first, then sell more, then improve efficiencies even more and then sell even more. Over time, speed up the back and forth between efficiency and selling until the two happen simultaneously.

Making your company more efficient is about more than just nixing extra coffee breaks and redlining your expenses. To tap into the river of profit flowing just under the surface of your company, you need to look at efficiency in every aspect of your business. Serving the same types of (great) clients with the same or very similar problems, using your one consistent solution to fix the problems, is the route of efficiencies. You want to duplicate your best clients, because that means they have a consistent need; and in turn, you want to reduce the variety of things you do to the fewest that will best serve your best clients' needs. Think McDonald's. That company is a moneymaking machine because they feed hungry people—who don't care, at least in the moment, about their health as much as their hunger—with a few products: fries, hamburgers and breaded chicken. The fewest things you can do repetitively to serve a consistent core customer need—this spells efficiency.

I want you to set a massive goal for yourself. Look at every aspect of your business and determine how to get two times the results with half the effort. That's a biggie, so I will say it again:

How do you get two times the results with half the effort?

Effort is financial cost and time cost (your time, your people's time, your software's time, your machine's time). For example, if you own a snowplowing company and currently plow one parking lot per hour, I would ask you to figure out how to plow two parking lots (two times the results) in thirty minutes (half the time). Huge profits can had if you can pull this off—rivers flowing, my friend. Rivers flowing.

Your first thought might be, "That's impossible, Mike!" (You wouldn't believe how often I hear this. Wait. Maybe you would.) If you believe that it's impossible to increase efficiency in this way, you are trapped in "let the other guy figure it out" mode. If instead you say, "Hmm. . . let me think about that. Let me find a way," you will skyrocket to profitability. Why? Because innovation occurs in small steps, big leaps and everywhere in between. To double the results with half the effort is a big goal that forces big thinking, and it brings about small and big progress—all of which goes to the bottom line.

The biggest innovators ask big questions. Do you think Elon Musk asked, "How do I get a few extra miles per gallon?" when he thought up Tesla? Or, "How can people transfer money a little bit faster than a bank wire?" when he started PayPal? As he worked on his Hyperloop supersonic speed-train concept—the one that travels through a complete vacuum system running from LA to San Francisco—do you think he was considering how to be a little bit faster than the Greyhound bus? Hell, no! Innovation in business and innovation in efficiencies comes from big, bold questions.

Most entrepreneurs focus only on tiny improvements—"How do I do this a couple of minutes faster?" Small questions yield small answers. Plowing a parking lot five minutes faster is not going to make much of an impact on your bottom line. Just skip the coffee break, or just "hold it" when you need to go to the bathroom.

But the more you focus on substantially improving efficiency (like with a design for a plow that can move snow twice as fast), the closer you'll get to achieving double the results with half the effort. This gain in efficiency is amplified the more you sell. That is the power of percentages. Since you now plow every parking lot more efficiently, every new account is an opportunity for increased profit.

Did you know that United Parcel Service (UPS) trucks almost always take right turns? In 2006, UPS dared to ask the efficiency question about fuel costs. They discovered that the less time UPS drivers spent in left turn lanes, the less fuel they burned waiting at lights and to cross traffic, and the less idle time there was for each driver. UPS is now experiencing a savings of $6,000,000 a year from the change.

The "brown truck" company didn't stop with their first efficiency discovery. Next time you see a driver delivering a package, look at him and try to spot his keys. Let me give you a hint: They are not in his pocket (that's a banana). UPS drivers found that fumbling for their keys in their pockets when they got back into the truck cost them five to ten seconds (or more) every time. UPS figured out that it is more efficient to keep their keys hanging from their pinky fingers. Now, a UPS driver makes a quick flip of his wrist and the keys are in his hand. Multiply that saved five to ten seconds by fifty stops a day and five gazillion drivers and you have a very huge savings indeed.

UPS also found that they could save millions by washing their trucks once every two days rather than every day. Over time, this gave them huge savings in time, energy and water—and the trucks looked just as shiny.

Look, it may seem impossible when you first hear my challenge, but if you've never asked yourself, "How can I get two times the results with half the effort?" how will you know if you can? You might be missing your own no-left-turn, pinky-flip, don't-wash-yourself efficiency miracle and not even realize it.

FIRE BAD CLIENTS

If you read my book *The Pumpkin Plan,* you know that, while the book is outwardly marketed as a system to help business leaders grow their companies into industry giants, it's secretly a book about efficiency. Letting go of clients who suck us dry and eat up our profit margins is a way of making space for clients we can serve exceptionally well by doing what we do best and with fewer resources. It is all about improving not only the top line, but the bottom line, too.

A study facilitated by Chicago-based growth-consulting firm Strategex analyzed the revenue, cost and profit breakdown for a thousand companies. What they found was nothing short of a "duh" moment, as in the "Duh, I already knew this but I still haven't done anything about it in my own business because I'm a glutton for punishment"-type duh.

Strategex sorted the clients for each company into four sections, in descending order based on revenue. For example, if a company had a hundred clients, the twenty-five clients that generated the most revenue were put in the top quartile, the next twenty-five highest revenue-generating clients in the second quartile, and so on. Strategex found that the top quartile generated 89% of the total revenue, while the lowest quartile only accounted for a meager 1% of total revenue.

Wait. It gets worse. The study found that each group of clients required pretty much the same amount of effort (cost and time). This means that it took the same amount of effort to serve a big-revenue client as it did a client who barely affected revenue at all.

Then came the awkward "gulp" moment. Strategex's profit analysis showed that the top quartile generated 150% of a company's profit. The two middle quartiles were effectively break-even, and the bottom quartile, the one that generated 1% of the total revenue, resulted in a profit *loss* of 50%! In the end, the profits generated from the top clients are used, in part, to pay for the losses accrued in serving the bottom clients.

I'm sure you know this scenario all too well. Those clients who barely pay you peanuts, yet constantly complain about how much you charge and how you do nothing right; the clients who demand you rework everything you've done for the third time and then never pay you for your work, or never pay you on time—those clients are costing you money. Get rid of them. Fast!

Dumping your worst clients may seem counterintuitive at first. But never forget what I said earlier: All revenue is *not* the same. If you remove your worst, unprofitable clients and the now-unnecessary costs associated with them, you will see a jump in profitability and a reduction in stress, often within a few weeks. Equally important, you will have more time to pursue and clone your best clients. I've lost count of how many readers have shared their stories of how both their top line *and* bottom line improved after they implemented the growth strategies I revealed in *The Pumpkin Plan*. I know that sounds like bragging, but it's not. The system isn't some miracle that I came up with; it is just simple math.

I know how scary it feels to dump any client when you are scrambling to cover this week's payroll, especially if you fought hard to get that client in the first place. But remember, profit is about the percentages, not a single number. So take it easy on yourself. Start by dumping one rotten little pumpkin in your patch, the one you occasionally fantasize about leaving on a deserted island or shipping off to Mars. The emotional distraction that client caused you and your staff will disappear immediately. The profits you earned from other clients and were spending to keep this bad client on board will now stay in your pocket. And since his special requirements no longer need to be serviced, you have time and headspace to find another, better client—an ideal client, a clone of your very best clients.

CLONE YOUR BEST CLIENTS

Just for a moment, I want you to think of your favorite client: the call you will always take, the person or company you say yes to without hesitation. This is the client who pays you what you're worth, on time, without question. This is the client who trusts you, respects you, and follows instructions. This is the client you *love,* and they love you. Now imagine if this client had five identical twin companies that all wanted to work with you. Wouldn't that boost your business? Wouldn't it be easy to serve those clients? Wouldn't it help you keep your bottom line healthy? Now imagine ten clones, or a hundred clones.

For almost any B2B business in the world, landing a hundred clones of their best client would put them at the front of the pack. They would dominate. The same is true for B2C businesses. If just a mere 10% of their clients behaved like their number one client, those businesses would rule, too.

Having clients with similar needs and very similar behaviors offers a few magical profit-making benefits:

1. You will become super-efficient, because you now serve very few but consistent needs, rather than an excessive array of varying needs.

2. You will love working with your clones, which means you will naturally and automatically provide better service. We cater to the people we care about.

3. Marketing will become automatic. Birds of a feather flock together (for real) and that means your best clients hang out with other business leaders who have the "best client" qualities you're looking for. Your best clients are awesome, remember? You love them and they love you, and that means they will talk you up every chance they get.

Clones of your best clients are the very definition of efficiency, which is why they are like gold. Find them. Nurture them. And then find out where even more best-client clones hang out and cultivate them, too.

SELL SMART

I mentioned Ernie briefly already, but I want you to know a little more about his story. It speaks to how fast things can go down the "upselling" rabbit hole. In the fall, I pay my lawn service to come clean up all of the leaves in our yard. This past year, Ernie, the owner of the business, knocked on my door. He had just finished the leaf clean-up and said, "I noticed that there are leaves in the gutters." He offered to remove them, for a fee. And I, my friends, was what they called a "captive customer" and an "easy upsell."

I said, "Yes, do it," without any hesitation.

Ernie had just expanded his service offering. Easy money. Yippee.

To complete the job, Ernie had to run out and buy some ladders for his truck. He came back thirty minutes later and got right to work. Because he pulled out the leaves by hand, he wasn't super efficient, but he got it done fast enough. However, he didn't have the tool to snake out the downspouts, so he made a note to buy it and come back at a later date to finish the job.

While Ernie was up on the roof, he spotted another opportunity—fixing damaged shingles. More easy money! More revenue! Again he asked me, I said yes and he ran out and picked up some roofing tools (and a downspout snake tool thingy). He came back an hour later, replaced the shingles, cleaned the downspouts—and, while doing that work, noticed a crack in the chimney and a soft spot on the roof, a sign of rotting wood. When Ernie approached me about it, I asked him to fix those things, too. This time he went out to get more tools, band saws, cement, brick supplies and temporary labor. Ernie came back near the end of the day and pushed through to get it finished. He even bought floodlights to keep the work area lit as dusk approached.

At the end of the day, I paid $1500 for all the work. Not a bad deal, considering Ernie "only" gets paid $200 to clean the lawn. But... the $1500 he earned cost Ernie an investment of about $2000 for tools and supplies that day, plus a lot of driving back and forth and the cost of hiring a laborer.

Ernie lost money on me, but he grew his sales by a lot. Tomorrow he intends to use his new equipment and tools to take care of other clients and will, in theory, earn his money back and then some. The problem is, that rarely happens. As the bills mount, the pressure grows to sell more and more; and you end up working on projects in which you have limited experience and sometimes little interest.

As the variety of things you do increases, you need to buy more tools and equipment and hire more specialized labor. And none of this gets used to its maximum potential, because you do many different things, not one thing. Your stuff sits there unused. While you rake lawns, your ladders just lie there. As you fix roofs, the leaf blowers just sit in your truck.

You get stuck in the Survival Trap and end up not doing a very good job at any one thing. For example, when Ernie wrapped up for the day he said, "I'll be back early tomorrow to clean the lawn again."

Why? Because he threw the leaves from the gutters onto the lawn he had just cleaned, as well as shingles and other things. His additional work required that he actually *redo* his original work, while all that new gear he bought just sat on his truck, not being used. What's efficient about that? Nada.

Across the street, my neighbors Bill and Liza hire a different guy, Shawn, to clean up their leaves in the fall. He also charges $200. On the same day Ernie worked on my house and earned $1500, Shawn serviced four more properties and also knocked on the doors at two other properties that, by the look of their lawns, needed his help.

I suspect that if Ernie and Shawn had had a beer together that night, Ernie would have boasted about doing one-and-a-half times the sales Shawn pulled, but Shawn would have ended up paying for the drinks. Shawn has achieved efficiency, and recognizes it as the magical sauce of profitability—getting more of the same things done with better and better results, using fewer and fewer resources.

Selling more is the most difficult way to increase profits, because in the best-case scenarios, the percentages stay the same; and in the worst-case, more common scenarios, expenses generated to support sales increase *faster,* resulting in smaller percentages and a smaller profit margin.

• • •

A man went in search of the perfect picture frame at a flea market in Adamstown, Pennsylvania in 1989. He found it holding a torn painting of a country scene. When he got home and dismantled the frame, he determined that it was not salvageable. But something else was.

Folded and hidden in the backing was the Declaration of Independence. Five hundred official copies had been used to spread the news of America's independence to everyone in the twelve colonies, and John Dunlap had printed this specific copy on July 4th, 1776. The man who found it took actions both to sell it and to remain unidentified. I'm not surprised—that $4 frame purchase turned over to 2.4 million dollars two years later, when it was sold by Sotheby's to a private investor.

The guy looking for the frame is a success by any measure, right?

He found the money under the surface. But if you think of him as a success, you're wrong. Sure, stumbling across success is cool, but making a *process* for finding profits under the surface is the real success.

This guy figured out that there is potentially big money hidden in frames. But if he only *hopes* to find another historical document one day, he is hoping for it to rain, not pursuing efficiency by identifying regions where such documents originated and searching flea markets only in those areas, focusing on frames made during a specific time period and buying inspection tools to look through the frames to see if there is anything inside. Can you imagine combing the flea markets without these and other efficiencies in place? He'd go broke trying to find that elusive rare document, trying to make it rain.

Sales without first putting efficiency measures and systems in place is a dangerous game that only leads to bigger expenses and fewer ideal clients. Applying efficiency strategies to your top line—firing bad clients, cloning the good ones, refining your offering to get the most out of your resources and then selling smart—is a surefire way to increase profitability.

ACTION STEPS
LET GO OF DEAD WEIGHT

Step One: Focusing on one aspect of your business (one that benefits your best customers), challenge yourself to figure out how to get two times the results for half the effort. Just pick *one* component and figure it out. Set a goal of accomplishing this task for a different aspect of your business every week, until you've looked at the full scope of your company and found ways to ensure you are running it with maximum efficiency. Shoot for the stars and you just might hit the moon.

Step Two: Using the parameters outlined in this chapter, identify your weakest clients. Fire the weakest links. I'm not suggesting that you get into 'Take This Job and Shove It" mode. Don't burn any bridges. Just politely end the relationships. You're not dating anymore, but you can still be friends.

8 STICKING WITH IT

As I write this, we're having a mother of a bad winter here on the East Coast. I hear other parts of the country also have it rough, but I've been snowbound in my house for what seems like eighty-four years, afraid to turn on the Weather Channel in case I might finally, permanently lose my mind. I'm not sure which state has had the worst of it, but while my heart feels it is Jersey, I'm pretty sure it's Minnesota. Actually, I'm convinced it's Minnesota.

The other day I caught up with Anjanette Harper, one of my best pals and the best damn writer on this planet, who lives across the border in New York. We were trading war stories over the phone about how the latest storm had affected each of our towns when she said, "Mike, I survived a mile-long hike in the Minnesota Northwoods… in January. We were sent out in waist-deep snow with nothing but a compass, some matches and a bag of granola. This winter has nothing on me."

Anjanette went on to tell me a hilarious story about Camp Widjiwagan (yes, that's its real name), a winter camp she attended with her classmates near Ely, Minnesota when she was thirteen.

"It was ridiculous—we were this group of private school kids from the city sent to an environmental camp way up north during the coldest month of the year. We weren't allowed to use the one indoor bathroom except to brush our teeth—seriously, the toilet seat had duct tape over it—instead, we had to put on three layers of clothes plus outerwear to trek out to the biffies (outhouses) in the woods to pee. I could barely walk in all of those layers, and it seemed like the biffies were miles away. I'm surprised my eyeballs didn't get frostbite. Just try going to the bathroom in the middle of a pitch-black night on a frozen toilet seat in a tiny wooden shack, with two active wolf packs howling at each other nearby."

I laughed so hard as Anjanette went on to tell me about a blind hike on a frozen lake (soundtrack: wolves!), building a *quinzhee* (an igloo), and putting up with earnest environmentalists who had no sympathy for the plight of pubescent teenagers not permitted to wash their hair. But it wasn't until she explained how the counselors managed to get the campers to change their wasteful habits that I realized I *had* to share her story with you.

"The first night, after we had dinner, we were asked to scrape the leftover food on our plates into a bucket. I assumed it was because they wanted to feed our scraps to some special breed of pig that could survive in the tundra, but then I saw the scale. One of the counselors weighed our combined leftovers and announced that we had managed to waste several pounds of food.

"Being a bunch of privileged brats, we responded with, 'Yeah, so?'

"And then we were lectured about how a few pounds of waste, repeated daily, adds up to a few tons of waste, and soon enough that adds up to a few landfills full of waste. Next, we got the ultimatum: We had to get the waste-per-meal down to a few ounces by the end of the week. I can't remember what the exact consequence was if we didn't pull it off, but it was something outrageous, like forcing us to square dance. . . with each other."

Anjanette went on to explain how, in the days that followed, she and her classmates held each other accountable for the amount of food they left on their plates at the end of each meal. They strategized and came up with solutions—the most important of these was to take smaller portions to begin with.

"We helped each other out," Anjanette explained. "If, after I was done eating, I still had vegan mashed potatoes on my plate and Ted and Brian wanted second helpings, I would pass them my leftovers. We nudged each other (or shouted at each other, take your pick) when our plates were piled too high with food. Toward the end, when it looked like we might not reach our goal, we really put the pressure on each other. Because, let's face it—we'd just hit puberty. We would have done *anything* to avoid having to touch each other, much less partner up for a square dance."

By the last dinner, Anjanette and her fellow campers surprised even themselves—they got that bucket down to zero waste. Zero. Zilch. Squat. As in, no one needs to do anything with the two words that should never be said together. . . square and dance.

When I asked Anjanette if any of the eco-friendly lessons she learned at Camp Widjiwagan stayed with her, she said, "I still turn off the water when I brush my teeth. And I'm more likely to shop for a few days' worth of groceries rather than stock up, because I despise throwing out food. So yeah, it stuck. I mean, I never want to see a snowshoe again, and the only school event for my son that I ever intentionally missed was the square dance; but it did change the way I think about using our natural resources."

In essence, what Anjanette and her friends did was form an accountability group to ensure they met their goal. I'm a huge fan of accountability groups because the benefits are numerous. Chief among them:

1. When you go through a painful process with others, the pain is diminished.

2. The action of enforcing a plan or system with someone else ensures that you are more likely to do your part. You are accountable to the group, and therefore *integral* to the group, which means you are less likely to drop the ball.

3. When you meet regularly with an accountability group, you get into a rhythm that makes it easier to stay the course and achieve your goal. Big aspirational goals get broken down into smaller achievable milestones.

The worst enemy of Profit First is not the economy, or your staff, or your customers, or your mother-in-law. Well, maybe it is your mother-in-law. . . but I digress. The worst enemy of Profit First is *you.* The system is simple, but you have to have the discipline to implement it consistently. If you do this, your company will be profitable, no question about it. The problem is, we are own worst enemies. We won't do the Debt Freeze all the way (or at all). We won't cut back on our staffing expenses or move into a grade-D office space. And we *will* steal from ourselves, taking money we allocate for profit to pay bills. We will steal from our Tax Accounts to pay our own salaries. We'll borrow. We'll beg. We'll steal (from ourselves). And we will find a way to justify it all, at least to ourselves. This is why it is imperative that we join (or start) an accountability group… immediately. Otherwise, there will be hefty consequences to our actions. . . and I guarantee they won't be as easy to face as forced square dancing.

ACCOUNTABILITY GROUPS WORK

Thomas Edison said, "Genius is 1% inspiration and 99% perspiration." I'm sure he would agree that success with Profit First is also 1% inspiration and 99% perspiration. It is in doing that things get done, and in sticktoitenacity (yes, I made up a word) that results are achieved.

And I'm convinced Jean Nidetch would agree with good ol' Edison.

Nidetch founded Weight Watchers in the 1960s, not with the intention of creating a wildly successful business, but with the goal of fixing a problem. (Isn't that how most great companies begin?) Throughout her childhood, Nidetch struggled with her weight. The problem continued and, by age thirty-nine, she weighed 214 pounds. Nidetch sure as heck didn't wear her weight like bikini model Amazon Eve, either.

After a run-in with a neighbor at the supermarket, Nidetch was finally motivated to lose weight. As the story goes, her neighbor complimented her on her appearance and then asked, "How exciting! When are you due?"

Not pregnant, Nidetch decided enough was enough. She started a diet recommended by a nutritionist and lost 20 pounds. Then, like so many of us, she lost her resolve.

Realizing she needed help, Nidetch reached out to several of her friends who were also trying to lose weight and founded a weekly support group. With the help of the group she lost another 52 pounds. All her friends lost weight too. That group eventually became Weight Watchers.

Nidetch celebrated her ninetieth birthday in 2013, having enjoyed more than fifty years of good health thanks to a sound nutritional system for losing weight and an accountability group to help ensure that she met her goals and never gained the weight back.

The science behind losing weight is simple: Consistently eat fewer calories than your body burns. Just as with Profit First, however, if your resolve falters, the system falls apart. This is why everyone—including me, including you—needs an accountability group. I don't care how disciplined you are, at times your willpower will fade. You need other people who are working the same system to help you stick to it during your toughest times, and will help you to help others do the same.

Weight Watchers meetings are facilitated by trained leaders using an established curriculum. These leaders have lost weight following the Weight Watchers system. They don't just teach it, they live it.

The fact that accountability groups work is nothing new. In fact, churches use them to help keep members focused on their faith. In *The Power of Habit* by Charles Duhigg, he explains how Rick Warren, a Baptist pastor, created his congregation. When Warren realized that his weekly motivational sermons were not enough to keep people focused on the lesson during the week and better able to meet challenges, he implemented small Bible study groups. His sermons were reminders of the lessons of their faith (a system of its own) and the small groups helped his congregation to stay focused on the lessons and implement them in daily life. Soon, 95% of Warren's church activity was happening during the week, in the small accountability groups.

Incidentally, Thomas Edison was part of accountability/mastermind group with Henry Ford, Harvey Firestone and John Burroughs. They called themselves "The Four Vagabonds," and though the group began as a camping tour, it was really much more. Together they mastered entrepreneurial domination and the ever-elusive secret trick to making a perfectly toasted marshmallow.

Knowing Profit First is only 5% of the game. To win it, you need the other 95%—and you'll get that in your accountability group.

GET STARTED

By now you know my philosophy on getting started—why wait? Do it now! To make it easier for you to get involved in your own accountability group, I've outlined the types of groups you could join, or start.

PROFIT ACCELERATOR GROUPS

Profit Accelerator Groups (PAGs) are facilitated by Profit First Professionals (PFPs), financial professionals or business coaches who are trained in the Profit First system, use it in their own businesses and help other entrepreneurs and leaders to implement it in their own companies. PAGs meet monthly or quarterly, face-to-face, at a Profit Center, at your (or another member's) facility or at their own dedicated facility. Some meetings take place over online videoconferencing.

PFPs have established, proven track records in fiscal/business management; they are accountants, bookkeepers, business coaches, business attorneys, financial planners and bankers. They also have access to the latest Profit First resources and know how to use them. PFPs enforce accountability and profitability; facilitate the sharing of best practices; and direct members on debt reduction, cost reduction and building efficiencies.

Why is working with a PFP an advantage? It's like working out with a professional trainer—you're going to get where you're going faster and more safely and efficiently. PFPs can guide you through the nuances of applying Profit First to your business, drawing on their expertise in working with many types of businesses and sets of special circumstances. PFPs have gone through this process many, many times, and that cumulative experience means they have already seen all the roadblocks you will face and are well-equipped to help you get around them.

If you would prefer to work with a PFP outside of an accountability group, most of them work one-on-one as well. PFPs do charge for their time, but man-oh-man is it ever worth it. Debra Courtright, the bookkeeper I mentioned in Chapter 1, is a PFP. She runs accountability meetings in her office; I was a member of one of the groups and met in her office for more than a year. No surprise, the entrepreneurs in her groups get to their financial objectives faster than most business leaders I've met.

Accountability works. Having a professional give you good shortcuts specific to your business works even better—it accelerates your profitability.

Michael Agulario of Gold Medal Services runs a $25,000,000 company and is in a PAG facilitated by his PFP, an accountant. One of the added benefits Michael's PFP brings to the group is, he offers to be the "bad cop" in vendor negotiations. Michael brings his PFP along to every meeting with vendors who are expensive but necessary to an efficient, profitable business. Then, Michael plays "good cop" while his PFP plays "bad cop" in order to get the best deal—sometimes saving hundreds of thousands in the process.

For example, after a pitch from his Yellow Pages sales rep, Michael said, "Sounds great. I want it."

But his PFP went all "bad cop" and said, "Michael, this is ridiculous. You can't afford this, or justify it. I want you to cancel the service."

Because Michael conceded to his PFP, the sales rep offered a lower price—slicing his Yellow Pages bill by $500,000! And he got double the run time for his ads. This negotiation is no different from any other, but Michael stays the "good cop" and can remain on friendly terms with his vendor.

For a list of PFPs, including those who run PAGs in your area, visit MikeMichalowicz.com/Resources.

PROFIT PODS

An alternative to joining a PAG run by a PFP is to join or start a voluntary Profit Pod. These groups are led by Profit Leaders, entrepreneurs who decided to start a Profit Pod as a way to help themselves remain accountable and help their colleagues do the same. While Profit Leaders do not run financial businesses, are not business coaches and have not been trained in Profit First best practices, they do have a passion for profitability.

The format for Profit Pod meetings is open source, but there are rules. Profit Leaders may not charge for the meetings except to cover any outright, documented costs (such as Meetup.com fees, room rental or food), and they may not solicit your business (nor may any of the members solicit business from other participants).

Because Profit Pods are open source, they are one hundred percent independent. To find one in your area, search the web, check out Meetup.com, BigtTent.com, Mightybell Circles or Facebook groups, or ask in entrepreneurs' forums. Group members enforce the Profit Pod rules, so if you're not happy with how a particular group is being run, give them an honest critique and leave the group. Then join a new Profit Pod, or better yet, start your own and run it the right way.

PROFIT LEADERS

Becoming a Profit Leader and starting your own group can be a fantastic way to ensure you not only are accountable to the Profit First system, but also are gaining the most from knowledge and experience as you tweak it to suit your company's needs.

At a recent speaking engagement on a local college campus, I asked my friend JB Blanchard to join me. JB had implemented Profit First in his roof-decking company, RoofDeck Solutions, Ltd., and wanted to share his experience with the students and professors in attendance. As we hustled over to the event, we passed a classroom.

JB pointed into the room and mumbled, "There he is. There's the best student."

Because I was mentally rehearsing my speech, I didn't ask him what he meant by that.

We walked by another classroom and he blurted, "There's the best student," pointing into the very full room.

That got my attention.

As I turned to ask him his criteria for identifying the best student, JB pointed into another classroom and said, "Over there, that woman. She is the best student in the room."

I stopped walking and looked at JB. "What are you talking about? How can you pick out the best students so quickly?"

"Easy," he said. "The best student is always the teacher."

Ahh, yes. This is why we teach—to learn, and to master. This is, in part, why Weight Watchers has such an amazing track record helping people lose weight and keep it off. Jean Nidetch, the founder, doesn't run the meetings or conduct teleconference after teleconference. No, her best members are the facilitators—her best students are the teachers.

Profit First is no different. If you want to master Profit First for your business, you need to teach it. Become a Profit Leader.

To make it easy for you to start your own Profit Pod, I've created a structure for you to follow (see below) and a *Profit Pod Starter Kit,* which includes instructions and core guidelines for how the meetings are run. You can download your own free copy at MikeMichalowicz. com/Resources.

STARTING A PROFIT POD—JUST TWO

The fastest Profit Pod to start only has two members—you and one other entrepreneur. The meetings are easy to manage and are over quickly. However, with a group this small you will not have the input of a financial expert or the power of input from a group of people. (Note: You cannot do this with a business partner or anyone who has a vested interest in your business.)

Everyone knows that you're more apt to show up to the gym if you have a workout partner there waiting for you. You might even work harder because you are there with your partner. But don't pick just anybody—your Profit First buddy has to want profitability as badly as you do. They have to "get it." Without shared values, passion and determination, meeting up with your Profit First mate would be a bit like meeting your workout partner at Dunkin' Donuts.

So pick someone who wants a healthy, profitable business just as much as you do. Better yet, find someone who wants it *more*.

When you partner up, become champions for each other. Yet be aware that, when there are only two of you, it is easier to get away with little white lies. We say, "Yes, I put the money into the account," when really we only *intended* to put it in, but never followed through.

The goal of accountability is to be integral to your Profit First system, not to punish each other for doing (or not doing) certain things. Instead, look for ways to improve discipline and cheer each other on for following the system. For example, you may decide that, rather than tell each other you made the deposit, you will email screenshots of your bank accounts to each other before your meeting or, if you're meeting in person, bring a print-out.

A Profit Pod of just two should meet on the phone, Skype or face-to-face twice a month. It's best to meet on the 11th and 26th (or whatever convenient day comes soon after you do your 10/25 Rhythm). When you meet, share your profit status; discuss any problems; share tips and tricks you have found for improving profitability and sticking with it; and hold yourselves accountable to tasks that will drive profitability.

Here's how to form a Profit Pod with just two members:

1. What you want in a partner is someone you already know but are not friends with. Inviting friends to join your group can lead to some messy stuff. I get it—you know your friends. You go way back. You want them to succeed. But trust me when I say that including your friends in your Pod is not the way to maximize the experience. You need honest communication between members who have no reason to be jealous or hurt, or to gossip to mutual friends about what they might have heard you share in the meeting. So choose a business acquaintance, someone you know delivers on commitments (that way you will be less likely to break yours).

2. If you prefer to work with someone you don't know, look online. Search Google for "Entrepreneur Online Forum" for a list of forums, and when you find one that is particularly active, post an inquiry in the forum for an accountability partner. Be very specific about what you want to do (e.g., have a call every two weeks, support each other in profitability, etc.). One of my personal favorites is The Fastlane Forum, managed by entrepreneur and business author MJ DeMarco. Interview prospects the same way you would a potential hire, asking whatever questions you feel are necessary to ensure confidence in this person. Be smart. Get references.

3. Another option is to post a tweet or Facebook status update: "I am looking for an accountability partner to focus on business profits." You will find some amazing people, and by using this method you will be able to weed out people who are interested but not committed. When I posted this same message on Twitter, two people responded with interest within a few minutes. I deliberately did not respond—after all, a good accountability partner is persistent. You know what? I never heard from those two people again. And just like that, they were off my list of potential partners.

Here is the core structure for running a Profit Pod with two people:

1. Schedule biweekly meetings around the 11th and 26th to correspond with your 10/25 Rhythm. A key factor in maintaining a successful Pod is to schedule your meetings a full year out, and then schedule your life around them. If you wait until you are both available to meet, you won't meet often enough for the group to work its magic.

2. Even with just two members, choose who will lead the agenda. The agenda for a fifteen-minute meeting is as follows:

a. Instant Profit First Check-In: In turn, each partner asks, "How healthy is your business?" and the other partner replies with a one-sentence assessment.

b. Three-Minute Update: Partner One gives a three-minute update about her business, including the thing(s) they agreed to be accountable about from the prior call, with no discussion.

c. Profit First Report: Partner One gives an update on current balances in her Profit Account, Tax Account and, if you have agreed to share the information, the Owner's Pay Account. Also, Partner One reports how much money was allocated to each account since the last meeting. This is the ideal time to email a screen shot of the relevant balances, to avoid cheating yourself.

d. Challenges Report: Partner One shares any struggles she may be having in allocating funds, and any potential problems or roadblocks that may be coming down the pike. If there are no challenges to report, simply say so.

e. Wins! Report: Partner One shares new "wins" and findings that may have happened in her business since the last meeting (e.g., ways to increase profits, methods for better adherence to Profit First, new sales, new processes, increased Profit First percentage, etc.).

f. Discussion: To get clarity, Partner Two asks Partner One up to three questions about her challenges and then asks for commitments to solutions. Partner Two then asks up to three questions about Partner One's wins, and for commitments to how she will repeat and grow them. The goal here is not to give advice or fix each other's problems; it is simply to put accountability in place.

g. Now, flip.

h. In turn, Partner One and Two each close with a commitment of up to three actions to further serve the health of their companies. Confirm the next call and get to work.

3. Every quarter, when you take a distribution, acknowledge your partner. Share how you plan to celebrate with your profits, no matter the amount. Give each other a virtual high five. Discuss ways to improve your accountability. The outline above can get boring quickly if you simply repeat it at every meeting, so think about ways you might freshen up the process. For example, you might start reading a book together. (Cough. *The Pumpkin Plan.* Cough.) When you have your call every two weeks, discuss another chapter from the book and how you will (or won't) implement the ideas.

STARTING A PROFIT POD/PROFIT ACCELERATOR GROUP—THREE TO TEN

A group of two members is easy to form, but if one person misses a meeting or starts to slack, the group is done. And, with only two members you are limited to input from. . . well, just the two of you. There is power in numbers. With three to ten members you have input from several people, and you have a chance to rotate Profit Leaders. Phil Tirone, my friend the former mortgage lender and founder of 720CreditScore.com, founded my accountability group. There are ten of us in the group, and though Phil got us started, he doesn't lead alone. We rotate leadership responsibilities every quarter, and this process has truly elevated the group. It also breaks us out of doing the same thing all the time. These groups have the feel of advisory boards.

Starting a Profit Pod or PAG of three to ten members can be a bit like herding cats. And if your group starts networking and conducting business together, things can go sour. So be sure to clearly state the rules of the group and make sure that everyone abides by them. Many PFPs facilitate groups of this size, so consider joining one of these professionally-run groups and getting their direction on running your own Pod.

You can use the same tools for finding your members detailed in the section above. Also, if you are in an existing group, consider plugging Profit First accountability into your existing core structure. For example, I have been a member of Entrepreneurs' Organization and in a forum (a blend of a mastermind and an accountability group, typically six to ten men and women) for fifteen years. We added Profit First to our group's agenda—a simple fifteen-minute plug-in—and it's been working well for everyone.

As is true of groups with only two members, the goal of the group is to work with other entrepreneurs and business owners who are committed to building profitable organizations, supporting each other in the process and holding each other accountable.

Here is the core structure for how to run a Pod or PAG with three to ten people:

1. After participating in accountability groups and masterminds of all sizes I have found that, for what we need to achieve, the best format is quarterly face-to-face meetings and biweekly rapid-fire check-ins (see core structure above for the rapid-fire check-in agenda). The biweekly check-in (45 minutes long) is necessary because business changes constantly. All of our wonderful plans go out the window when a client suddenly goes bye-bye, and we need the biweekly check-in to make adjustments and deal with challenges. The quarterly meetings allow for a deep dive to support each other at a much more tactical level.

2. First Meeting: When a new group forms or a new member joins an existing group, it is critical to establish a strong, deep connection immediately. Now, before you say this can't be done, try getting stuck in an elevator with someone you don't know for an hour—you will become best of buddies for life. It can be done; it just needs to be structured correctly. Allow an hour and a half for a first meeting if you are meeting often, and if you are doing a deep-dive group, allow four hours.

3. Master Exercise: I will never forget my first deep-dive accountability meeting back in 2011. Our group decided we would start with an exercise called "Full Financial Disclosure." I call it "Getting Naked." We agreed to walk into the meeting with our tax returns, bank statements, loan statements, credit card statements—all that stuff we normally wouldn't want a business colleague to see. Talk about a bonding exercise!

4. No Business: You may not do business with each other. You can refer work, you can help each other, and you can give freebies if you must (I suggest avoiding that), but no matter what, no money changes hands. Not only do things go sour if there is a problem (and it will affect the whole group), but complete honesty also goes away because your vendor or client is now in the room.

On my website, I share detailed examples of agendas for first meetings, check-ins and deep-dive meetings. To download the agendas, visit MikeMichalowicz.com/Resources.

PROFIT CENTERS

After I started centering some of my speeches on Profit First, large businesses approached me. They wanted in. From my early conversations with these businesses, an idea was spawned for Profit

Centers: locations in which small and large businesses provide free space for face-to-face PAG and Profit Pod meetings. Many banks, for example, have conference rooms (and lollipops). Some corporations have auditoriums (and lunchrooms). What better way to have a meeting than at one of the bank branches? After you wrap up the meeting, you can each walk up to the teller and make your Profit First deposit, or your quarterly withdrawal for your Profit First celebration!

Then other corporations approached me, wanting to offer discounts on their products and services. They realize that a Profit Pod represents great clients for them (hey, big business needs to be profitable too), and that it is effectively a small buying club.

For a current list of Profit Centers, visit MikeMichalowicz.com/Resources. If you don't see a conference meeting space in your area (or services and products that you want at a lower cost point), simply contact me and we will work to get one listed.

KEEP THE GROUPS HONEST!

In Dan Ariely's book *The (Honest) Truth About Dishonesty,* he explains how we lie to everyone, including—or, says Ariely, especially—ourselves. In short, he explains how, if given the opportunity, most people will cheat a little. Few people are big cheaters—the kind you see on *America's Most Wanted*—but everyone is a small cheater. We call our cheats "little white lies" to soften the truth and make ourselves feel better about cheating, but it's still cheating.

Weight Watchers meetings kick off with a weigh-in. You step on the scale and the facilitator notes your weight; you are the only two people who see it. There is no public embarrassment, but also no opportunity to lie. Ultimately, you come out winning because you can't lie to yourself.

You can't lie with Profit First, either—not to your peers and not to yourself. This is how we make sure small cheats and little white lies don't happen in a PAG: Each member must bring the printed-out statement from his Profit Account to each meeting. (Or, if you are meeting online, send a screenshot via email.) Numbers do not lie, even if we are tempted to do just that. (Just a teensie-weensie bit.)

Just as it works with Weight Watchers, you don't need to show your number to the entire group. You just need to share it with your PFP if you're in a professionally facilitated PAG. If you are in a volunteer Profit Pod, your group needs to designate one person to be the number validator. By sharing this indisputable evidence with one person other than yourself, you won't be able to lie to anyone (including yourself).

• • •

My friend Anjanette is the sarcastic sort, and she likes to tell a funny story. But when she came to the end of her tale about Camp Widjiwagan, her tone changed. We had been talking about this book, and about how I had already decided I wanted her to let me share her story with you as an example of how accountability groups can help people stick with the program. She agreed and said, "You know, Mike, I joked about it, but the thing is, that trip to Camp Widjiwagan changed my life."

When I asked how, she explained that she had always been the pudgy girl—the kid picked last for teams, the girl who faked a stomachache to get out of running the mile to save herself the embarrassment of always coming in last. She said that at Widjiwagan, everything changed. She tried to do every physical task they threw at the campers, even though her classmates didn't expect her to do anything.

"On one of the last nights, they took us on a trail through the woods to this cabin and taught us about the constellations. Then they said, 'Now we're going to separate the boys and the girls and go jump in a hole in the ice.' I was gobsmacked! Apparently we were expected to strip down to our wool socks, sit in a scorching-hot sauna and then run out in the snow to a hole in the ice where two counselors would dunk us in the freezing cold lake.

"When the counselors asked who wanted to do it, it was crickets. No one wanted to try it. I mean, at thirteen years old our first thoughts were probably, 'NAKED! WHAT? ARE YOU CRAZY?' The room was quiet and I thought, 'Anjanette, if you don't do this you will regret it for the rest of your life.' So ever so slowly I lifted my hand in the air and said, 'I'll do it.'

"My friends were shocked. They thought I was joking. But when I stood up and followed the counselor to the door, they knew I was serious. Now, because I was the girl who sat out every game, every run, every tennis match, they all felt compelled to follow suit. It was an, 'If Anjanette is doing it, that means we have to do it'-sort of thing. So in a way, I was their accountability leader. I held them accountable to the experience and they fell in line."

Anjanette paused to collect her thoughts. Then she said, "It was amazing, Mike. Jumping into that hole in the ice, totally naked, not caring what anyone thought of my body. And being the first one to do it—that was huge. It set the tone for the rest of my life. I'm a risk-taker now. And it's partly because I decided to lead. As a leader, by default I held *myself* accountable."

To secure the success of Profit First in your business, to really lock it down and ensure that your business will be profitable *beyond your comprehension,* you must hold yourself accountable to the process by whatever means necessary. Lead a group or join a group. Either way, you will achieve levels of profitability you would never hold yourself accountable for alone.

And look at it this way—at least you don't have to jump naked into a hole in the ice on a twenty-below-zero, January Minnesota night. Anjanette would tell you that it's not so bad, anyway. She'd say, "It's better than square dancing."

ACTION STEP
HOLD YOURSELF ACCOUNTABLE

The Only Step: Start looking for a PAG or Profit Pod that will meet your needs, or start your own. Begin that process TODAY! For a list of PFPs who lead such groups, or who can help you start one, visit the Resources tab at www. MikeMichalowicz.com. No matter what, don't go it alone; it's much easier to stay the course when you do it with others.

PROFIT FIRST —
ADVANCED TECHNIQUES

9

WHEN folks first join Weight Watchers, they set a goal of losing 10% of their body weight. Even if you weigh 300 pounds and have to lose another 150 to get down to your ideal weight for optimal health, you still only set a goal of losing 30 pounds. The strategy is to string together a series of small wins and build momentum, plain and simple; and it's the reason why Weight Watchers has such an impressive success ratio compared to other diet programs. With 10% of your body weight kicked to the curb you can focus on the next 10%, and then the next until you get down to your ideal weight.

If on the other hand you focus on the target weight loss goal of 150 pounds from the get-go, you will likely become discouraged and give up; it takes a long time to lose an entire person! Massive goals feel exciting when you declare them, but can quickly become de-motivating factors because they seem so hard to reach and the chance to celebrate is so far off in the future.

You'll see a lot of formerly overweight and obese people getting into running marathons and triathlons and other extreme endurance races and sports. Do they start this way right out of the gate? Heck, no. They start with a walk around the block. Then a longer walk. Then maybe a walk-run cycle. Then maybe they sign up for a 5K.

Small wins lead to big wins, and if you started implementing Profit First back in Chapter 3, you already know that. You lost your 10% and ran your first 5K. Now you're ready to take on the advanced stuff. Like a dieter who recently completed a few small goals, your business is healthy enough to take on bigger challenges, now, much healthier than it was before you first cracked this book.

Here's the deal: you are about to learn the Profit First equivalent of running your first marathon. You need to be in shape and all stretched out before you do it. So please do proceed with reading, but don't implement this stuff until you have completed at least two full quarters with the core stuff you learned about Profit First. Are you making your biweekly allocations? Are you amassing some profit, no matter how small? Have you experienced a few profit distributions? Are you participating in some form of PAG? If you answered yes (a *real* yes) to all four, if you've mastered *not* breaking the rules, you're good to put on your running shoes and move forward.

ADVANCED SIMPLIFICATION

A few years after implementing Profit First for myself, I realized that I could really take my money management to the next level if I tweaked my system further. The stuff I taught you in the beginning of this book was working well, but there were certain times I still needed to do the accounting work to understand the financial health of my business. Sometimes my deposits weren't made as a result of sales; they were simply reimbursements for expenses. Other times, a client paid a wad of cash up front for work that I would do in dribs and drabs over the next year. Sometimes I needed to make big purchases, and I wanted to save for them. Mine wasn't the only business that needed tweaks; everyone I consulted with needed them. So do you. And the process is simple. You need just a few more accounts.

While it may not seem like opening additional accounts simplifies anything, it absolutely does. Whenever you can get a clear, accurate picture of how much you have to spend on a specific aspect of your business, you will make better decisions and be less likely to commit to projects, vendors and expenditures that do not fall in line with the balances in those accounts. Likewise, if you know exactly how much cash is flowing into your business at any given time, you can make better decisions about where you need to focus your efforts.

You already have your four foundational Profit First accounts open—Profit, Operating Expenses, Owner's Pay and Tax—plus your two no-temptation accounts that don't get touched, the Profit and

Tax Accounts in a separate bank. Here are the additional accounts, contingent on your business needs, that I recommend you consider opening:

INCOME ACCOUNT

This is probably the most helpful and important account for advanced Profit First. I can't imagine your business not benefiting from it. In this account, you collect all of your income deposits so that you can clearly see how much cash you collected between your 10th and 25th allocations. This will separate incoming from outgoing cash, both of which were being managed by the Operating Expenses Account in the simple version of Profit First.

An Income Account will give you an accurate picture of how much money you collected during any period of time. And the Operating Expenses Account will transition to only paying the expenses for operations, so you will have an accurate picture of how much money is flowing out of your business at any given time.

It's critical that you adjust to your Real Revenue. If you have material and subcontractor costs, allocate these fixed amounts first, before you do the percentage allocations. Then, on the 10th and 25th of every month, allocate *all* remaining money in the Income Account to the other accounts: Profit, Owner's Pay, Taxes and Operating Expenses. And possibly a few others suggested below.

THE VAULT

The Vault is an ultra low-risk, interest-bearing account that you can use for short-term emergencies. At a certain point, leaving 50% in your Profit Account to act as a rainy day fund is not prudent since the money flow is a little unpredictable. A bad quarter won't contribute much to the Profit Account. Then you take 50% out for a profit share, and now that Profit Account reserve might be too small for a big business. Every business should have a three-month reserve, meaning that, if not a single sale came in, all costs could still be covered for three months (a quarter). The question isn't *if* you will have a dark day (your supplier goes out of business, your biggest client goes bankrupt, your best employees leave to start a direct competitor and your clients decide to go with them, etc.). The question is, *when* will your dark day come? The Vault is there for that.

When you set up The Vault, you *must* also establish certain rules for its use. What I mean is that, when you have a situation so dire that you need to access this money, you also have instructions written in advance on how to proceed. For example, if the money is pulled due to a drop in sales, you will pre-plan that, besides just trying to get more sales, you will also cut all the related costs in your business within two months if things haven't improved. Few people have the discipline to think clearly or act appropriately in times of panic, and that's why we document a simple set of instructions for ourselves in advance.

The idea behind The Vault and the entire Profit First system is that it puts your decisions well out in front of any money crisis. Your business dynamics may not, in fact, improve; but your decision-making will be much farther out in front of the actual financial impact. So the goal of The Vault is *not* to buy time; it may afford some time to address unexpected challenges, but it is really about forcing important decisions early, so your business doesn't go into a cash crisis (you know, back to the Survival Trap).

STOCKING ACCOUNT

This is an account for big purchases and to fund stocking parts of your inventory. For example, remember my friend JB? His roof decking company, RoofDeck Solutions, Ltd., sells the materials contractors need to complete their projects. JB includes some basic nuts and bolts with each order, usually fifty or a hundred of each; yet his supplier requires a minimum order of ten thousand at a time, which costs JB roughly $5000. Each order will last JB ten months or longer, so he set up what he calls a "large purchase account" into which he allocates 1/20th (that's $250 each time) of the funds he will need for the next big nuts and bolts purchase. Why 1/20th? Because he knows he'll need the next order in ten months, and he is on the 10/25 Rhythm. Ten months, two times a month, equals twenty allocations before the next big purchase. By doing this, JB is able to chip away at the big bill *before* it happens. Then, when it's time to cough up the $5000 for the next big nuts and bolts order, he's ready. In the past, this bill caught him off guard and he had to scramble to cover it. Now, he barely feels the $250 he allocates to his Stocking Account twice a month.

PASS-THROUGH ACCOUNT

Some businesses receive income from customers that is not to be allocated for Profit or Owner's Pay. Sometimes you may provide a service or a product to your customer at cost (or near cost), and other times you may be reimbursed for costs outright. For example, I travel a lot for my work and in almost every case my clients reimburse my travel costs. That income is not allocated to cover payroll or added to my Profit Account. It's a pass-through and goes directly into this account, and then off to the corresponding vendor to pay the bill. If I have paid the bill in advance, the money is deposited into the Pass-Through Account and then transferred (on the 10th or 25th) to the Operating Expenses Account, from which I paid the initial bill. By the way, with all these advanced accounts, the nickname you give each is entirely up to you. I call this one my Reimbursement Account.

MATERIALS ACCOUNT

If most of your revenue (as indicated in the Instant Assessment) falls into top line revenue and does not flow through to Real Revenue, then most of your income is pass-through revenue and the core of your business is basically the management of that pass-through. If this is the case, set up a Materials Account for the money that is allocated specifically for purchase of materials. Do not allocate it for anything else. (Ever!) If for some reason there is money left over at the end of the quarter (in other words, you had a larger profit margin than you expected), you can move that balance to your Income Account (or Operating Expenses Account, if you aren't doing advanced Profit First yet) and make the allocations accordingly. The Materials

Account functions in the same way the Pass-Through Account does, but it is broken out separately so that you know its exclusive purpose is for materials.

SUBCONTRACTOR/COMMISSION ACCOUNTS

If your business does not purchase materials, but uses contractors or people paid on commission instead, this is where you allocate the funds to pay these fine folks. Treat it just like the Materials Account, but apply it to contractors and commission-based team members.

EMPLOYEE PAYROLL ACCOUNT

Employee pay is relatively predictable—full-timers are on salary and part-timers, for the most part, work an average number of hours per week. This means you can look at the cumulative gross pay for your employees plus the payroll taxes you'll incur and allocate funds from your Income Account (if you use advanced Profit First) or Operating Expenses Account (if you use basic Profit First) to the Employee Payroll Account every 10th and 25th. If you use a payroll service, set them up to pull the payroll from this account (not your Operating Expenses Account).

MAJOR EQUIPMENT ACCOUNT

Similar to your Stocking Account, this account is for big purchases you may need to make farther down the road, such as new computers or a high-end 3-D printer. Estimate how much you might have to spend on future equipment purchases, divide it by the number of months you have to save up for it, divide that number by two and allocate that amount every 10th and 25th to accumulate enough money for that big purchase.

DRIP ACCOUNT

This account is for retainers, advance payments and pre-payments on work your company will complete over a long period of time and for which you have yet to expend resources. Say you get a big project (congratulations, by the way), and you receive $120,000 from the client up front for work you will complete every month over the period of a year. That means that each month, you will really be earning $10,000. So when you get that check, put the $120,000 into the Drip Account and then automatically transfer $10,000 to the Income Account every month (or better yet, $5,000 every 10th and 25th). You don't touch any of the balance in the Drip Account. You only make allocations when you drip a portion of the funds—in this case, the $10,000 each month—into the Income Account.

The Drip Account will help you manage the true cash flow of earned money, so that you can manage your expenses and costs. For example, the labor doing the work will be paid monthly. I helped implement a Drip Account with my friends at TravelQuest International in Prescott, Arizona. They provide their clientele with once-in-a-lifetime trips, from viewing solar eclipses from the best vantage points in the world, to visiting the South Pole to see the Aurora Australis, to experiencing zero gravity in outer space. People book these trips up to five years in advance, while the majority of the company's expenses occur during the year of the event. Enter the Drip Account.

PETTY CASH ACCOUNT

Set up a bank account and get a debit card for petty cash purchases, such as client lunches. Then, allocate a regular dollar amount from your Operating Expenses Account to petty cash. Me? I allocate $100 every two weeks for myself, and also for a few employees who need it. The funds cover gifts, lunches and other small purchases. Sorry—if I'm buying, we likely aren't having an eight-course meal. . . if it's not in my Petty Cash Account, it ain't in my budget.

SALES TAX ACCOUNT

If your business collects sales tax, every single, stinkin' penny of the sales tax you collect is immediately allocated to this account. For example, if you sell something for $100 and sales tax is 5%, you will deposit $105 into your Income Account. First, transfer that $5 into your Sales Tax Account; then do your Profit First allocations with the remaining $100. Sales tax isn't even legally your money; you are just acting as a collection agent for the government, so never, *ever* treat that money as income. Just bang people over the head for the sales tax and turn it over to the king (the government).

Figure 7 is my own account setup. The account numbers are made up, of course, and the balances are not my real numbers. But they do show a very typical breakout of the cash, and the names of the accounts

BANK 1 (For My Business Operations)

NAME	ACCOUNT	BALANCE
Income	**3942	$13,432.23
Profit (15%)	**2868	$0.00
Owner's Pay (31%)	**0407	$4,881.88
Tax – Gov't Money (15%)	**4365	$0.00
Operating Expenses (39%)	**5764	$3,767.18
Petty Cash ($75)	**4416	$142.66
Employee Pay ($1,500)	**8210	$1,845.46
Reimbursement (0%)	**4247	$212.58
Drip (0%)	**8264	$27,500.00

BANK 2 (So My Temptation Is Removed)

NAME	ACCOUNT	BALANCE
Profit	**1111	$14,812.11
Tax – Gov't Money	**2222	$5,543.91
The Vault	**3333	$10,000.00

Figure 7: Mike's Account Setup

are the real names I have assigned to my accounts. Next to each name, in parentheses, I put either the dollar amount or percentage that goes into each account at the allocation times (the 10th and 25th). You should do the same.

Looking at the numbers, I can see instantly where my business stands. I can run an Instant Assessment at any time. For the purposes of this example, I set my required personal monthly income at $10,000 per month. From there I can instantly calculate the total business income I need to make between every allocation period.

WRITE DOWN THE PROCESS

Create a single-page document that defines the function of each account. Explain what purpose each account serves, and the process you will follow. For example, document that, on the 10th and 25th of the month, all the money in your Income Account is distributed to the Profit, Owner's Pay, Tax, and Operating Expenses Accounts based on the respective percentages. Then, the specific dollar amounts—$75 for Petty Cash and $1500 for Employee Pay—are transferred from the Operating Expenses Account into the respective accounts. Finally, the total money in Bank 1's Profit and Tax Accounts are transferred to Bank 2.

This process is a system, so it needs to be documented. Your bookkeeper might have to take this over for you; otherwise, you might drink too much one night and forget the rules you set up for your accounts. Heck, you could end up allocating all of your money to your Erik Estrada Fan Club fund, a fan club of which you are the only member (even Erik dropped out).

PICK YOUR PAY TO FIND THE NECESSARY BUSINESS INCOME

The famed "monthly nut" is a horrible distraction. It's up there with reruns of *Jersey Shore*. The monthly nut is a remnant of the GAAP mentality that simply tells us the number we need every month to keep the doors open. And *that* is nonsense. The "monthly nut" is a focus on—you guessed it—expenses, not profit. The concept of the monthly nut makes you focus on expenses and do everything you can to earn your "nut" with enough sales. In other words, it has us put costs first and makes the goal to cover expenses, not to improve profitability. Can you say "Survival Trap?" Good. I knew you could.

You get what you focus on, so stop focusing on expenses. Focus on profit and the expenses will be taken care of by default. Screw the "monthly nut." Instead, focus on your Required Income For Allocation (RIFA). This is the money you need to deposit by the 10th and again on the 25th to have a healthy business, to pay the salary you want from your business and to take the profits you deserve. Period.

Take your monthly, required personal income and divide it by two, since you are getting paid twice a month. Then divide that number by the percentage being allocated in Owner's Pay. Using the (made up) amounts on Figure 7, I would divide $5000 by 0.31. The result is just over $16,000 in business income, which means that by the 10th and 25th of every month I need to collect and deposit around $16,000 into the Income Account to cover it. It's really that simple.

So when I look at my Income Account (above), I know instantly that I am currently falling short by $3000 and need to keep the sales moving. Every two weeks the Income Account drops to zero when it is allocated, and I need to rebuild it to $16,000 or more. Yes, there is a nice chunk of change in my Drip Account; but that money is for services I will render over another twelve months, so it will only account for about $1000 every allocation period. Using this system, my sales revenue minimum becomes very, very clear.

WHEN YOU HAVE MORE THAN ONE BUSINESS OWNER

Just one more point about Owner's Pay: If you have a partner or multiple partners who are also getting paid, you need to add up the total income requirements for the company. So if you need $10,000 a month and your partner also needs $10,000, the total owner pay is $20,000 per month. Divide that number by two; then divide again, by 0.31, and you get an RIFA of more than $32,000.

You may also notice that the Profit (15%) Account with Bank 1 is at zero. That is because it is simply a holding tray for a day or two. Money gets allocated from the Income Account and goes to the Profit (15%) Account at Bank 1. Then, on the same day, I initiate a transfer to Bank 2, to pull the entire amount of money out of the Profit (15%) Account at Bank 1 and put it into the Profit Account at Bank 2. That is where the profit accumulates. And I can see, it looks as though I will have a really nice, $7000-plus profit celebration at the end of this quarter. It's a simple calculation: $14,812.11 x 50%. Par-tay!

This same holding tray setup is in place for my Tax (15%) Account. Allocate and then remove the temptation immediately.

Also, you may notice that no bank summary "grand total" is shown in the table. The accounts aren't all automatically added up to show a total combined balance. Many banks do this for your convenience, but I suggest that you disable the option (if you can). The grand total of all your accounts shows you all the money on one big plate again— exactly the thing we want to avoid. Looking at a grand total messes with your mind, so don't do it.

THE PARETO OVERLAP

You may be familiar with the Pareto Principle, commonly known as the "80/20 rule." For the history buffs: Vilfredo Federico Damasa Pareto was an Italian economist. While studying the distribution of wealth in Italy in the late 1800s, he discovered that 20% of the Italian population owned 80% of the land. Then he looked at his garden, and observed that 20% of the peapods contained 80% of the peas. Then he looked down at his feet, and exclaimed, "OMG—I own five pairs of clogs, yet I wear these super-fly boots 80% of the time!" And *then,* out of nowhere the theme song from *The Twilight Zone* started playing, thus marking the first time that music was associated with a slightly unsettling a-ha moment.

Okay, okay. I made up that last part, but you get my drift. Pareto's pattern is everywhere. Eighty percent of the time you drive, you're cruising down the same 20% of the roads you'll travel in life. And, despite your love of the sale rack, you will still pull from the same 20%

of the clothes hanging in your closet, 80% of the time. Chances are, you are wearing one of your fave pairs of pants or shoes right now, as you read this. You are, aren't you? That's Pareto's rule at play in your own life. Cue Rod Serling and a smoldering Chesterfield cigarette.

Pareto's Principle also applies to your clients, in that 20% of them yield 80% of your revenue. This is a foundational principle of the growth strategy I detailed in my book, *The Pumpkin Plan*. And it goes further—80% of your profit is derived from 20% of the products and/ or services you offer.

The key to this advanced strategy is to connect the two—your clients and your offering. Some of your top clients buy most of your profitable offerings; some of your top clients go for the offering with the lowest profit margin. Likewise, some of your weakest clients consistently purchase your profitable stuff and some are just weak all the way around, buying the same no-profit stuff over and over again.

Once you see the overlap, the decisions become very easy. Get rid of the "bad" clients who only want your least profitable products and services. You are losing money here, catering to clients or customers who are not a good fit for your company.

Find a new way to manage the weak clients who do buy your most profitable offerings. Often, "bad" clients can become better clients if you meet with them to set new expectations and methods of communication. Meet with your top clients who don't buy profitable offerings, too. Find out how you can deliver profitable stuff to them.

When you focus on profit *first,* even when choosing the clients and customers you are willing to work with, you increase your profit dramatically. Not only do you save money by cutting expenses related to serving weak clients, who don't buy profitable offerings; you also free up your time, energy and creativity to focus on the clients you love, who bring in the profit. Applied to your client base, the Pareto Principle is an advanced Profit First technique that does double duty— you save money *and* gain profit. Gotta love that!

And those beloved top clients, who routinely buy profitable offerings? You are going to rock their world. Get to know them better than they know themselves. These are the clients and customers you want to clone. Remember, profit is in productivity. Systematize the overlap of your best clients buying your most profitable offerings and watch your Profit Account grow by leaps and bounds.

EMPLOYEE FORMULA

There is a really simple formula for determining if you can afford a new hire—or if your business is currently understaffed or overstaffed. For each full-time employee, your company should generate Real Revenue of $150,000 to $250,000 (ideally more, but this is the minimum). So, if you want a million-dollar company, you know that you can afford four to six employees (including yourself). This is just a ballpark number; every business is unique. But do not use your super distinctive status as an excuse to hire more people.

Efficiency is always the goal. Always. Not hiring your husband's cousin who is down on his luck and "could really use a job." Not finding space for the brilliant kid who has a ton of great ideas you could use… someday. You're a "bottom line" person now, remember? You flipped the formula. Now, you're working the "Sales – Profit = Expenses" system. You're taking profit first. And that's why you're forced to be careful with your expenses.

And remember—we're talking about Real Revenue, not top line revenue. Subtract your Material and Subs cost *before* you divide by the magic number range to get to your ideal employee count.

Again, this is not an exact, perfect system, but it will give you a better and more realistic understanding of what it means to be over- or understaffed. The reason these numbers aren't perfect is because labor costs vary tremendously. A guy cooking French fries at McDonalds will make much less than the lady who engineered the next generation smartphone. In this example, cheap labor is less costly but also has a smaller impact on revenue. The fry guy just facilitates that sale of fries, and the engineer creates an entirely new product and revenue stream.

Remember Greg Crabtree, the author of *Simple Numbers, Straight Talk, Big Profits* whom I met an entrepreneurial award event? I had a call with him one evening. After he poked fun at Virginia Tech (my alma mater) losing to Alabama (his alma mater) yet again, he shared another instant labor analysis he agreed to let me pass on to you.

According to Greg, your Real Revenue must be two-and-a-half times the total labor cost if you're running a tech business. This is because the tech industry traditionally requires expensive labor (highly-trained people who have a big impact on revenue). If, on the other hand, you are in a "cheap labor" field, such as the fast food restaurant example I used above, your Real Revenue must be four times your total labor cost.

For example, let's say you're a manufacturer with $6,000,000 in Real Revenue. If you hire "cheap labor" (like assembly line personnel), you will divide $6,000,000 by four to get $1,500,000. This means that your total labor cost (the people on the floor and the folks in the office) should not exceed $1,500,000. And if you are a manufacturer with $6,000,000 in Real Revenue but use "expensive labor" (like scientists and engineers), divide the $6,000,000 in Real Revenue by two-and-a-half to get a total labor cost of $2,400,000.

MINI POWER TACTICS

Some advanced Profit First strategies require very little time and are super effective. I am constantly tweaking and improving my system, so if you want to know about my latest discoveries, and share yours, visit my blog at Mike Michalowicz.com. Here are my favorites (so far):

THE GOVERNMENT'S MONEY

It's so easy to "borrow" from our Tax Account. (It's really stealing, but you don't need me to tell you that... oops. I just did.) The money is just sitting there, taunting us with all of those zeros we could put to good use. When we cave and pull from the Tax Account, we don't feel the pain right away. But when tax time comes, we can get in *really* big trouble. Owing more taxes than we have money to pay means that, at a minimum, we'll be paying interest and possibly penalties on the amount we owe.

A smart tactic is first to move this account to a third-party bank that you don't see, and then change the name of the Tax Account to

"The Government's Money." Now, I suspect that, like me, you would be *way* more reluctant to "steal money from the government" than you would be to "borrow money from the Tax Account."

HIDE ACCOUNTS

Following the "out of sight, out of mind" theory, you are less likely to justify transferring or withdrawing funds from your accounts if you can't see them. Some banks allow you to "hide" accounts so that you can't see them on first view when logging in to online banking. Try hiding all of your accounts except for the Operating Expenses Account. You can still do the disbursements and the entire Profit First system using this tactic; it just means that now you won't consider the other accounts when making spending decisions.

OUTSIDE INCOME ACCOUNTS

Chances are that as your business matures, you will add a variety of other accounts that collect income. You may have a PayPal account to collect funds, or a wire account for international business or local transfers. The challenge with these accounts is, you might start to view them as "extra," like your own additional petty cash fund. They're not extra. They are part of your revenue, and you need to make sure that you protect and allocate the funds just as you would any deposit into your main bank account.

For this tactic, set up all your outside income accounts so that any income is transferred to your main Income Account on a daily basis. Some banks will let you set up an auto-transfer for the total balance in the outside account, which is ideal as long as you keep whatever minimum balance is required to avoid extraneous administration fees.

If you can't do this automatically, simply transfer the money to your Income Account when you do your biweekly allocations. Just note that these transfers may take a few days, so you won't instantly have the money in the Income Account and will have to wait until your next allocation period to move the money to all the individual accounts.

ACCOUNT SNAPSHOT

To keep track of your accounts, set up auto-notifications for your key accounts via email or text. Have the bank report the balances of your Income Account and Operating Expenses Account to you on the 10th (when all of your money has accumulated) and the 15th (when all of your money has been allocated and all checks have been mailed; and again on the 24th (accumulated) and the 30th (allocated). Set up a daily notification of the balance in your Petty Cash Account. Check the other accounts manually.

This quick report will ensure that you are acutely aware of how cash flows in (Income Account) and what is available to go out of your business (Operating Expenses Account) and out of your own spending allotment (Petty Cash).

BANK CHECKS

Until we see that a payment has cleared, we still think of the money is ours. And sometimes we forget we wrote the check. Hello, insufficient funds charges and a ticket straight to the ninth circle of hell. This technique changes that dynamic immediately. Rather than pay with checks you write by hand and mail (if you don't lose the envelope on the floor of your car), pay with bank checks.

Also called "bank pay" or "bank payment processing," bank checks are processed by your bank quickly. More importantly, the bank will pull the money for the checks you "write" immediately. This way, you know the money is gone forever as soon as you process a payment.

Yes, the bank makes money on "the float," and you lose any interest you may have earned in the few days it would take your payment to be received and processed by vendors. But I say, "Who cares?" Here's the dealio: If you manage hundreds of millions or billions by processing checks and transfers manually, it's a good strategy to cling to your money for a few days because the interest earned on your operating capital in even just a few days is significant. But for most entrepreneurs, the interest earned in "the float" is embarrassingly negligible—usually around $5 per year, and you'll spend more than that on postage, mailing out your payments! So let the bank do the dirty work, why don't ya?

ACTION STEP
PLAN TO ADVANCE

Choose one of the advanced tactics or strategies detailed in this chapter and add it to your to-do list for six months from now. It may seem silly to add a to-do item so far out, but if you don't put it on your radar, you may end up forgetting that there are advanced strategies that could help you take Profit First—and your company—to the next level.

10 LIVING PROFIT FIRST

I'M going to Disneyland!

It's the iconic moment—a sports team wins the championship game and the field reporter rushes over to the star player to ask the same old question: "Hey, giant football guy, you just won the Super Bowl. What are you going to do now?" The player smiles, showing a big gap in his teeth, stares right into the camera and shouts, "I'm going to Disneyland, mother@#$%&!" The station beeps out the @#$%&! part. Barely.

I thought about this phenomenon during a recent conversation with Laurie Udy, accountant and owner of Secretly Spoiled, a company that recently started using Profit First. She shared with me that she took her family on their first Disney vacation using her quarterly profit disbursement. A type-A numbers person, Laurie had been investing everything she had in her business—most of her time and all of her revenue.

"I was living check-to-check," Laurie told me. "I wasn't taking a salary."

All of that changed as soon as Laurie started plugging Profit First into her well-organized system. Within months, her personal finances stabilized; and by the time her first quarterly disbursement came around, she had enough to take her family on their first trip to Disneyland.

"The trip was amazing, and we're already planning the next one," Laurie said. "But what really surprised me was, after funneling all of my money into my business thinking that it was the only way to make it grow, my business actually started to grow *faster* when I started paying myself and focusing on the profit first!"

Like so many of us used to "doing anything" to build our businesses (including going without pay and delaying profit indefinitely), Laurie had to learn how to give herself permission to use her hard-earned money not only to pay herself, but also to *enjoy* herself—to provide experiences for her family that would enhance their quality of life and create a lifetime of treasured memories. The business was no longer a cash-eating monster. Not even close. It said, "Bon Voyage!" to Laurie and her family as they cruised off to Disneyland, mother@#$%&!

This won't come as a shock to you: Everything you just learned about creating a Profit First business also applies to your personal life. I mean, if you think about it, running your life is like running a business. You generate income and spend money. Your income likely varies at times. You never know when a crisis might hit and make a huge dent in your bank account. And you have a vision for your life, just as you have a vision for your business—one that, before reading this book, you may have thought hinged on a lucky lottery ticket or some other sudden windfall.

Now you know better. You know that in order to save enough money for a rainy day and the celebratory pleasures of life, you need to pull that money out before you spend a dime on other things. You know that a smaller plate will help you trim the fat from your lifestyle and zero in on what's most important to you and find fun, creative solutions to get what you want. And you know that the big vision you have for your life does not have to hinge on luck or fate—it can be earned, not with a dollar for the Powerball, but with a simple change in habit, practiced consistently.

You know what? That's a big, big deal. And I want to acknowledge it. I want *you* to acknowledge it. This small change you made, putting profit first, is the entrepreneurial equivalent of winning the World Series, the Super Bowl and Stanley Cup. You created the miracle that is your business and now, by implementing the Profit First system, you have ensured its greatness—not just in terms of profitability, but also in terms of the positive impact your business will have on the world.

So guess what? It's time to get your gappy, toothy smile on. *You're going to Disneyland!* Let's apply your championship-winning strategy to the rest of your life, okay?

THE PROFIT FIRST LIFESTYLE

The ultimate goal of the Profit First Lifestyle is financial freedom, which I define as doing what you choose to do whenever you choose to do it. Financial freedom means that you have reached a point where the money you've saved yields enough interest to support your lifestyle and continues to grow. The path to financial freedom is paved with simple, small habit changes that become systematized and apply to both your business and personal finances.

Now, I did not write this book to teach you about your family budget or your 401K, but I do know this: If you own a business, your personal financial health is in lockstep with the financial health of your business. In fact, the analogy of your business being your child is only partially accurate. A better analogy is that your business is your Siamese twin. Separating yourself from it must be done with absolute surgical precision, and even if the operation is successful you will always share a soul.

So, soulmate, you need to apply everything you're doing right now (and planning to do) to fix your business with Profit First to your life, too. I wrote this chapter to serve as a take-action-now primer on living a Profit First life. I suggest you also read David Ramsey's *The Total Money Makeover*. If there is a Bible for getting your personal finances lined up the right way, I believe his book is it. And who knows, maybe down the road I will write my own "New Testament."

That said, here is the core stuff you need to know about setting yourself up to live a Profit First life:

1. Face the music. This step should be easier now that you've faced the truth about your company's finances. Add up all of your monthly bills, plus your annual bills and the debt you owe.

2. If you have any debt at all, stop accruing more. Put a freeze on all purchases you cannot pay for with cash.

3. Establish a personal Profit First habit. Set up an automatic withdrawal so that every time you get paid, which should now be twice a month on the 10th and 25th, a percentage immediately transfers into a retirement savings account. If you are carrying any amount of debt, keep the retirement percentage at 1% until the debt is paid off. Use every penny you have after necessary expenses to eradicate your debt.

4. Set up your "small plates." Create four core accounts and multiple Day-to-Day accounts.

   a. Income Account. This is the account into which you make deposits. From this account, allocate money to the other accounts.

   b. The Vault Account. Initially, this is the "oh shit" account, the amount of savings you must have on hand to get through the month if—scratch that—*when* something dire happens. Now, Suze Orman recommends saving eight months' worth of living expenses, but that's not doable for basically any human being on this planet, right off the bat. However, you will work toward it slowly and methodically—you know, Profit First style.

   A good starting balance for The Vault is one month's rent or mortgage payment. If you can spare that right now, transfer it to The Vault immediately. Remember, this account must be difficult to access (e.g., different bank, no online banking, no checkbook, etc.). Once you eradicate debt, The Vault will grow and grow, with the intention of having the cash you save here eventually become a source of income. This is where money makes you even more money.

c. Recurring Payments Account. This account is for payment of your recurring bills, including fixed (e.g., your mortgage or car loan), varying (e.g., utility bills) and short-term (e.g., an installment plan for your kid's braces).

Determine the monthly average for your varying recurring bills, plus 10%. Then total your fixed recurring bills. Add the two totals together plus the cost of your short-term recurring bills: This is the amount you will transfer from your Income Account into your Recurring Payments Account every month. If you have it, transfer that amount now.

d. Day-to-Day Account (multiple, if needed). There are many day-to-day costs in keeping a family running—groceries, clothes, school supplies, Girl Scout cookies, date night, running shoes, Girl Scout cookies, baby-sitting, toiletries, snow tires, Girl Scout cookies. . . sorry. If there is anything that can take me joyfully down the sugar high path, it's the ultimate in sweet delights: Girl Scout Samoas cookies.

Set up a Day-to-Day Account for anyone in the house who's responsible for paying for these types of expenses, and transfer the amount that each person needs every 10th and 25th from the Income Account, based on spending requirements. For example, my wife and I both buy stuff for the house—I'm the Costco king, she handles the grocery stores. And we both gas up cars and pay for kid expenses. Get a debit card for each person so that purchases are deducted from the account immediately.

e. Debt Destroyer Account. This account receives all remaining funds and goes toward eradicating debt. Following Dave Ramsey's advice, make the minimum payment on each debt. Then, regardless of interest rates (unless they are extreme), pay off your smallest debt first. Wipe that sucker out and then move on to the next one. Ramsey wisely says that paying off a debt, however small, creates a mental momentum that will motivate you to pay off the rest of your debt, faster. Remember, we are emotional beasts, not logical ones.

If you are carrying debt, I want you to cut up your credit cards. Remember, it's much easier to go with human behavior than it is to fight it, so removing temptation is the best solution.

However, I do have one exception. An entrepreneur's income can be highly unpredictable. You could have an amazing month followed by a zero-dollar month, followed by a not-bad month, followed by a why-do-I-bother month. If you follow Profit First, your Owner's Pay Account should address this and your income should become consistent. But in the beginning, it probably won't be. And if you're a start-up, you may not get any cash at first. For these reasons, I believe in keeping one credit card line to buffer you in dark months. Put the credit card in a sealed envelope labeled "emergency only" and give it to a trusted friend to hold onto. I am serious. You must remove temptation. Here's how you manage your emergency credit card the Profit First way:

Every quarter, as you make progress paying down debt, reduce your credit limit by 50% of the amount you paid down. Say you have a maxed-out card with a $10,000 limit. By the end of the quarter, you've managed to pay down $3000 of that debt (nicely done, my friend). Now you have $7000 in debt and a $10,000 limit. What I want you to do is call the credit card company and ask them to reduce your limit by $1500, which is 50% of the amount you paid down in the first quarter. Now your debt is $7000 and your credit limit is $8500. In doing this, you put up a guard rail of sorts, a mechanism to protect yourself and keep your debt total down (should you convince yourself it's okay to max out your credit card again), while keeping a credit line buffer in place should you need the card for emergency funds during slow months.

Keep following this method every quarter until your credit card balance is zero and your credit limit is $5000. Put that credit card in a sealed envelope and store it in a safe place (your wallet, it goes without saying, is *not* safe). Better yet, have a reliable friend hold onto it for you. This is your emergency line.

Now, for those of you who say, "But Mike, if I drop my credit line, my debt-to-credit-limit ratios will fall out of favor with lenders and my interest rates will go up!"

To that I say, "Who cares?"

The goal here is to remove financial stress from your life by eradicating debt, not to get better rates on *more* debt. We can worry about improving your credit score once you are debt free. Remember my buddy Phil Tirone? That's what he does now. Once he figured out the formula for becoming debt free, he started 720CreditScore.com, his business that repairs credit scores. Follow suit... first, destroy your debt. Then, fix your score.

RIP OFF THE BAND-AID

The day my daughter handed over her piggy bank in an effort to help solve my self-made financial crisis, I still had all three of my luxury cars parked in the driveway. I was still a member of the country club I never went to and had a ton of recurring expenses that, quite frankly and even more embarrassingly, I could not name.

In the weeks and months leading up to that moment, I knew I was running out of time, but still held onto the trappings of the lifestyle I had earned (but not "learned"), the lifestyle I thought I deserved and did not want to give up. But my daughter's amazing act of selflessness woke me up to the reality that none of that stuff mattered.

It's common for us emotional humans to give up the stuff we can no longer afford (or couldn't afford in the first place) by small degrees. We cling. We keep hoping that something will "turn up" and "save the day," and so we dole out the pain in small increments, biding our time. We do this because we hate loss. More specifically, we have a far greater desire to avoid losing something than we have to acquiring something. This behavioral response is called Loss Aversion, and it is mighty powerful. Combine it with the Endowment Effect—the theory that states that we place a much higher significance on something we possess than on an identical thing that we *don't* possess—and you are dealing with a stubbornness resembling that of a three-year-old in a tug-of-war for a beloved blankie. ("Mine!")

For example, the beautiful red Porsche you've been eyeing—it would be nice to have, for sure. But once you have it, it's way past "nice." Now, it's badass (and so are you). You polish the car. You take friends for rides in it. You take selfies with that red beauty in the background of each photo (just by chance, of course). You love it because now that you own it, your relationship to it has changed, even though it's the same car you once idly admired from the showroom floor.

Then you get the notice: You missed yet another payment. If you miss one more they will repossess your baby. *Your* baby. So what do you do? Return the car? No, you cancel your daughter's ballet class (she kinda sucked anyway), and your gym membership (you kinda sucked anyway), and that trip to the Cape (because everyone knows, anyone who goes to the Cape sucks... a lot). You eat ramen noodles every night. Shoot, you even cancel the insurance on the damn car and keep it parked safely in your garage until "better days" come along. So what if you can't drive it? At least you didn't lose it. At least it's still *yours*.

I behaved the same way. I cut back everywhere I could, but nowhere that I should have. Then, when I couldn't pay a bill and the credit cards were maxed, I cut just enough things to get by. The next month it happened all over again, only worse. Juggling bills and drumming up money were a source of constant stress.

The night after my "piggy bank moment," I remembered what I used to do in the past, when money was tightest in the early days of starting up a new business: I wouldn't cut expenses in ineffective dribs and drabs. I would cut them all.

It was time for me to return to what worked. It was time to rip off the Band-Aid.

I cut everything. The luxury cars? Gone. (I replaced the three cars with two used, basic models.) The swanky club membership? Gone. The little extravagances, like the Netflix account? Gone. And here is what made it easier—I realized that no one gives a crap. I mean truly, no one cares. I'm guessing you had no idea I was slashing and burning when I was in the throes, never thought for one second, "Hey, I wonder how good ol' Mikey is making out with his financials?" And I'll bet you aren't crying about me right now, either. And that's cool, because that's reality.

When you realize that 99.99% of the people who know you or know of you won't care what you own or where you hang out or what your circumstances are, and that the 0.01% who, for whatever reason, can't stand you will simply point a finger at you, laugh evilly and then direct their self-loathing misery at someone else, it's easier to ditch the pimped-out ride.

And when you realize that 99.99% of the people who *do* know you and truly love you will rally around your courage, as my family did for me, that, *that* is when you will stand up, brush yourself off and say, "Let's do it."

DEATH TO DEBT

Now, your business will be sending you a quarterly profit disbursement check. Yippee! Celebration time! And do you know the best way to celebrate when you have mongo personal debt? Have a death-to-debt party. It's super fun and goes something like this: As soon as you get your disbursement check, turn on some tunage that gets you fired up—my choice would be Metallica's "Seek And

Destroy," but if you don't have a mullet, do your thing. For God's sake, though, don't crank up the Barry Manilow or "Escape (The Piña Colada Song)" by Rupert Holmes… we want to destroy debt, here, not make love to it.

Then, make sure you have a glass of libation, or whatever floats your boat. Finally, take 90% of your profit disbursement and use it to pay down debt (smallest first). Call it in using your debit card, or go online and get it done immediately. Then, and only then, raise your glass and say, "Cheers to me!" Then, we dance (or swing our sweaty, stringy mullet hair around while listening to Metallica). The party is over in about ten minutes, but that debt? It's gone forever. Hey, wasn't that a total blast?

You may think I'm being sarcastic here, but I'm not. To me, paying down debt is *winning,* and winning is fun. Get yourself some of those crackers the Brits give out at Christmas—you know, the little cardboard tubes covered in wrapping paper that two people pull apart like a wishbone to reveal little trinkets and revelry inside?—for your party. Invite your spouse. Whatever it takes to commemorate the occasion. (And if you videotape your tiny death-to-debt party, send me a link, okay? I want to post the best of the best on my blog.

Use the remaining 10% of your profit disbursement however you please. Go out to dinner. If you don't have enough for dinner, go out for ice cream. No matter what your disbursement is, cherish it. Celebrate with it. Your business is still serving you and killing debt at the same time.

After you've eradicated your core debt—credit cards, bank loans and student loans—start using 45% of your quarterly profit disbursement to kill remaining long-term debt and keep 55% for your splurge item or experience. This is another psychological move. It's more gratifying to get the bigger chunk of the fruits of your labor and spend it on whatever the hell you want than to take the smaller chunk. So use 45% to expedite the payoff of long-term debt beyond your normal monthly payments (mortgage, car payments) and keep the rest for whatever crazy antics you get up to. (What? I don't judge. And I totally didn't see *anything.*)

After you own your cars and home outright and have wiped out debt from every nook and cranny of your life, one hundred percent of the profit disbursement goes to you. And this time the party had better be legit. I'm talking a band and some good booze, maybe stuffed pizza instead of plain. And my wife and I had better get an invite.

LOCK IN YOUR LIFESTYLE

Remember the graphic in Chapter 2 that showed how our expenses increase at a parallel to our income? That is the concept of Parkinson's Law (nothing to do with Parkinson's disease), in which C. Northcote Parkinson explained how our available resources (time, money) expand to fill the space made available for them. This is why, if you give yourself two weeks to complete a project, you will get it done in two weeks; but if you give yourself eight weeks to finish the same project, it will take eight weeks. This is also why, if you have ten dollars in your pocket, you will spend ten dollars. As our income increases, Parkinson's Law takes over and we spend every extra penny we earn.

Now that you know your salary and actually take it, you need to live within your means. Then, you're going to lock in your lifestyle. What that means is, no matter how good things get (and this is going to be a challenge for you, because now that you follow Profit First things will get *amazing*), you will not expand your lifestyle in response. You need to accumulate cash—lots of it—and that means no new cars, no brand-new furniture or crazy vacations. For the next five years, you will lock it in and live the lifestyle you are designing now so that all of your extra profit goes toward giving you that ultimate reward: financial freedom.

Don't freak out on me, now. I'm not telling you that you shouldn't go out to dinner with your sweetie or go away for the weekend. (Were you thinking a B&B? I like B&Bs.) You need to enjoy life. I get it. What I am telling you is, in order for Profit First to have a permanent impact on your life, you need to build as big a gap as possible between what you earn and what you spend. The more cash you can collect the better, because at a certain point money starts *earning* you substantial money, all by itself. Money yields interest and returns from investments. And remember, once the money you have collected yields more new money every year than you spend in a year, you have achieved financial freedom.

Here are five rules to help you stay locked in to your lifestyle for the next five years:

1. Always start by looking for a free option.

2. Never buy new when you can get the same benefit you would if you bought used. (It's used as soon as you buy it, anyway.)

3. Never pay full price if you can avoid it.

4. Negotiate and seek alternatives first.

5. Delay major purchases until you have written down ten alternatives to making the purchase and have thought each one through. Save your splurging for Profit First quarterly disbursements! Yay!

The Profit First Lifestyle is a frugal lifestyle, for sure. But the frugal lifestyle is not the same as a cheap lifestyle. You can and will live very well (actually better) when you are frugal than you would when you are posing as a big spender. Why? Because frugality removes financial stress, enabling you to better appreciate and enjoy the things and experiences you purchase. Big spenders buy the same things, but their purchases are served with a big ol' heaping serving of massive stress. Who's got time for that? Remember, well-dressed poverty is still poverty.

If staring down the next five years is too much for you, that's cool. I have a Plan B for you. (And if you do rock the five years, this is your next step after your locked-in lifestyle term is up). It's called the Wedge Theory, a term that has been floating around entrepreneurial circles for a while, which as far as I can tell was originally coined by Brian Tracey. The idea of the Wedge Theory is to only gradually (and mindfully) upgrade your lifestyle as your income increases. Every time your income increases, you set aside half of the increase in savings so that you don't expand your lifestyle to, as Parkinson's Law suggests, "use all available resources."

So for example, if you're taking home $100,000 (post-tax, paid by your business) and your Profit First Lifestyle means you're setting aside $20,000 every year and living on $80,000; this is where you will start your wedge. Half of every income bump over and above $100,000 will go directly into The Vault. The Vault starts piling up cash, and changes from a "Holy crap, I have no money" fund to a "Holy cow, that's a lot of money" fund.

Let's say your take-home income goes up to $135,000, an increase of $35,000 over the previous year. You would take 50% of the $35,000 ($17,500) and drop it into The Vault. This leaves just over $117,000. Because you live the Profit First Lifestyle, you now take 20% and set it aside for savings. With the increase in income, that number is now $23,400. That brings your annual savings up to right around $50,000. And, you are now living on more as well—$93,600, to be exact, an increase of more than $13,000. Your life moves forward, but the Wedge Theory, combined with Profit First, allows your savings to climb super fast, getting you that much closer to financial freedom.

PROFIT FIRST KIDS

When was the last time you got a chunk of free money? The answer is never. And even if you were granted money (thanks to old great-gramma Sally), there is always a tradeoff. Regardless of how you get your money, the universe seems to find a way to make us earn it. This is why I don't gift my kids an allowance. Instead, I set up a chore list with corresponding pay rates and post it on the refrigerator. (You can download one from the Resources section at MikeMichalowicz.com.) The kids decide how much they earn, by working for it.

Give your kids some mailing envelopes (you know, the snail mail type) and have them label each one:

1. One for the big dream, like my daughter's horse. Have them stash up to 25% of their chore money in this envelope.

2. One to help support the family. This number should be a recurring number, such as $5 a week to contribute to groceries or entertainment. The key is to have a recurring fee so they get used to having to pay out something on a regular basis. Make sure the number is age-appropriate.

3. One for impact. Have them put 5 to 10% into this envelope to give to a charity of their choice, or to use in a meaningful way... like starting their own business, one that both serves the community and makes money!

4. One for The Vault. This is where they will sock away 10% of their funds for a critical emergency (hopefully your kids will never have one, but you want them prepared from day one), which will also become an investing source as the money accumulates.

5. One envelope for mad money, to buy whatever they need or want—toys, music, books, etc. Let them earn money and have fun!

I mentioned my barber Lou in the Introduction. He is the master of the envelope system. He divides every day's take among envelopes appropriate for his business. His shop has been profitable every single month for decades and he has no debt (except he owes me a haircut for mentioning him in this book).

It goes without saying that the kids must follow the Profit First golden rule: Always allocate the money to the different accounts (envelopes) before doing anything else.

This system will teach your kids so much about the value of money—how to manage it, how to earn it, how to finance their dreams. It may feel strange at first (I'm talking to you, helicopter parents), and you'll surely get some pushback; but this is a massive gift to them. Imagine how your financial life might have turned out differently, had someone taught you these important lessons and strategies? Or, if you are lucky enough that your parents did, just think about how well it served you and do the same for your kids.

Giving your kid a car may feel nice to you, but it's selfish as hell. You are only avoiding "disappointing" your children when you indulge them and make their lives easier, and this only hurts them when they enter the "real world" completely unprepared for reality. Let your children get burned a little within the safety of your parenting, rather than scorched in the unsafe and often cruel world.

• • •

One of my favorite Profit First Lifestyle nights was when my wife and I and two of our friends went into New York City to see Jimmy Fallon at his former show, *Late Night with Jimmy Fallon.* The tickets were in a lottery and we happened to get them. We saw the show live, and laughed and laughed. Meatloaf opened the show and Twisted Sister ended it with a rocking three-song mini-concert. Seeing Jimmy Fallon cost a whopping zero dollars. Watching Dee Schneider bang out "I Wanna Rock" cost zero dollars. In the words of the famous commercial: "An amazing night out with my wife and friends? Priceless."

Here's the deal—living the Profit First life does not have to be excruciatingly painful. I'm not suggesting that you sell everything and live in a hut, work by candlelight and eat whatever you can find on the forest floor. I'm not even suggesting that you give up the things you love. I'm simply suggesting that if you want true financial freedom, you will have to let go of your preconceived notions about what you "need" and start placing a higher value on financial independence than you do on your stuff. It's not rocket science. And it won't kill you. Promise.

ACTION STEPS

LIVE PROFIT FIRST

Step One: Set up corresponding Profit First allocation accounts for your personal expenses.

Step Two: Based on your most recent pay and the "lifestyle lock" explained in this chapter, figure out how much you should truly be living on.

Step Three: Have a sit-down with your entire family and talk numbers. Tell them what you're doing with Profit First and the positive impact it will have on your family's long-term financial health. And if it helps, you can tell the kids that this method was something suggested by "Uncle Mikey."

WHERE IT ALL FALLS APART

11

I n the spring of 1954, the notion of any athlete running a mile in less than four minutes was considered impossible. Four minutes was the accepted top limit of human potential because up until then, the fastest measured mile was four minutes and 1.4 seconds.

Good thing Sir Roger Bannister didn't get the memo.

On May 6th of that year, history was made when Bannister completed the mile in three minutes and 59.4 seconds, breaking the world record and shattering the myth that no human being could run faster than a four-minute mile. Even more surprising was the fact that although Bannister had competed in the 1952 Helsinki Olympics, he had very little time to train for this world-record race as he was also working as a junior doctor at the time. Still, he pulled it off. Was it because he didn't get the medal he wanted in Helsinki and was driven to accomplish the "impossible" in order to redeem himself? Perhaps. Or was it simply because he believed it could be done, and he was the man to do it? Maybe.

Whatever gift or grace Bannister had working for him on that blustery day in England, one thing is for sure—the myth of human limit was replaced with the possibility of human potential. That Bannister shattered the myth of the four-minute mile being impossible to beat was proven just forty-six days later, when Bannister's rival John Landy broke his record, running the mile in three minutes and 57.9 seconds.

In working Profit First in my own business and helping entrepreneurs do the same with their own companies, I can tell you that the biggest hindrance to a successful implementation of this powerful plug-in is our own perception of limits. Even after we start working the Profit First system, we are vulnerable to tired myths about what works and what doesn't, what can be done and what can never be achieved.

Profit First falls apart when we buy into accepted notions of how financials "should" be managed:

"It takes money to make money."

"You'll make money at the end."

"If you want to make more money, you need to sell more."

"You just need to follow the accepted accounting principles. It's all there."

That last one is tough for most entrepreneurs to refute, because we hire bookkeepers, accountants and CPAs as experts. If they don't agree with the Profit First system, maybe we should go back to our old way of doing things. Right?

Ah. . . nope.

The other day I got a call from Bob, an accountant affiliated with one of the businesses I was hired to consult with (and, let it be noted, Bob is *not* a PFP). He said, "You know, Mike, all of these bank accounts you set up, they're a real pain in the ass. Each one needs to be reconciled, and there are constant transfers between them. All you need is one account. You can do all of these separate accounts on your general ledger. I mean, for God's sake, Mike—it is so easy to be profitable. Just do the accounting and all of this other stuff is unnecessary."

I blame my snarky response on a lack of sleep, because I don't get ruffled too often. I said, "Bob, you have about two hundred clients, right?"

"More like two-fifty."

"Wow, two hundred and fifty clients," I said. "And you do all of the accounting for them and prepare the tax returns and the P&L (profit and loss), the cash flow and balance sheets, right?"

"Yep. Of course, Mike."

"And I suspect you tell them exactly what you told me," I continued. "That they just need to do the accounting and look at the statements and it's all right there in black and white?"

"Yes, absolutely. Where are you going with this?"

"I just want to know," I replied, "what percentage of your clients are truly profitable. I want to know how many of your clients have a true chunk of accumulating cash sitting in their business at the end of each year. I would be shocked if it was even twenty percent."

Radio. Silence.

"Is it less? Is it ten percent?" I pressed.

Still no response from Bob, though I heard some heavy breathing on the other end (not the fun kind).

"Are you saying that, just following the logic of accounting, less than five percent of your clients are profitable year in and year out, Bob?"

Click.

"Bob, are you there? Earth to Spock. Earth to Spock. Are you there, Spock?"

If it all boiled down to conventional wisdom, you would be rich and every business would be profitable—and we'd still be running four-minute miles.

The fastest way to screw up Profit First is to start sliding back into old belief systems that got you into trouble in the first place. It's easy to do. The relief of finally getting a handle on our finances and watching our profit rise can cause us to feel that our little cash flow problem is "fixed" and we can go back to using old-fashioned accounting methods, focusing on the top line and dumping our money in one account. We think, "I get this now. I don't need to move money around to all of these accounts. I don't have to withdraw my profit first on *every* deposit."

That kind of thinking, my friend, is like starting down a slippery slope. I'm not sure why you would choose that over the smooth path, but again I'll just chalk it up to being human.

In this chapter, I'll share a few more pitfalls to avoid as you work the Profit First system. Chief among them is the willingness to fall in line with conventional thinking. Fight the urge! Since Bannister beat the four-minute mile, runners have knocked seventeen seconds off that time. Seventeen seconds! Surely you can run a profitable business—you won't even have to break a sweat.

GOING TOO BIG, TOO FAST

It is extremely common for entrepreneurs new to Profit First to start putting 20% or even 30% into their Profit Account right out of the gate. The next month they realize they can't afford it and pull the money back out to pay bills, which defeats the entire process. You must allocate profit and not touch it, so you've got to be sure that your business can handle the reduction in operating income.

To increase your profit, you need to become more efficient, to deliver the same or better results at a lower cost. Profit First works from the end goal backwards. Once upon a time, you used to try to get more efficient in order to turn a profit. Now, by taking profit first, you must become efficient to support it. Same result, reverse-engineered.

This is why I suggest you start with a small percentage. Don't fall into the trap of hogging all of the grub, taking too much profit up front and then shuffling most of it back into your Operating Expenses Account when payroll comes due. Start with a small percentage to build the habit. Every quarter, move your Profit First allocation percentages closer to your goal by increasing them by an additional one or two percent. Starting slowly will still force you to look for ways to get better and more efficient at what you do, but you won't be tempted to throw in the towel on the entire system because the pressure is too great or the task "impossible."

Remember Jorge and Jose, the Profit First masters of the greater Miami area? At one point, pumped at the results they had achieved with lower percentages, they allocated 20% to their Profit Account and quickly realized their business could not support both that much profit *and* the tremendous growth they were experiencing. So, they adjusted the percentage until they achieved a balance with their Profit Account allocation—high enough to make a real difference in their rainy day and celebration funds, but low enough that it did not hinder growth.

Jorge and Jose adjusted the Profit Account percentages on a regular basis, factoring in short- and long-term needs and delaying equipment purchases they couldn't swing. They did everything right—and have a successful, thriving business to show for it.

"Too much of a good thing" is possible, even when it comes to watching your Profit Account grow rapidly. Whether you make this mistake at the outset of implementing the Profit First system or down the road when the future looks especially rosy, be sure to correct it as soon as possible or you'll find yourself slipping back into the Survival Trap.

CUTTING THE WRONG COSTS

By now, you know I'm a renewed frugality junkie. I get a high from saving money, and I get the biggest rush when I find a way to eliminate an expense altogether. Still, not all expenses should be cut. We need to invest in assets, and I define assets as things that bring more efficiency to your business by allowing you to get more results at a lower cost per result. So, if an expense makes it easier to get better results, keep it or purchase it.

I once toured the factory of a company that makes knives. When I noticed they were using old tools, one of the owners said, "Yup. We even have systems from the 1960s! We save so much money by keeping our old equipment."

During my tour, I also noticed that the knives they produced were inconsistent in terms of quality. Some of the knives were sharp; some were not. The handles rarely had a snug fit. Coincidentally, I had toured a different knife company earlier that week and noted that in one cumulative hour of manufacturing time they were able to turn out one perfect knife after another at a volume four times that of the company stuck in the decade of screaming Beatles fans and free love.

Money is made by efficiency—invest in it. If a purchase will bring up your bottom line and create significant efficiency, find ways to get the same results with different or discounted equipment (or resources, or services) rather than cut the cost.

"PLOWING BACK" AND "RE-INVESTING"

We use fancy terms to justify taking money out of our different allocation accounts to cover expenses. Two that are used most often are "plowback" and "re-invest," which are really just other ways to say, "borrow." I have done this. I "plowed back" money from my Profit Account to cover operating expenses, and boy, do I regret it.

When you don't have enough money in your Operating Expenses Account to cover expenses, it is a big red flag that your expenses are too high and you need to find a way to fix them fast. Once in a blue moon, it could also mean that you are allocating too much to Owner's Pay or Profit. This only happens when you start with a high Profit or Owner's Pay percentage. And when it happens, it is because you are taking a percentage of profit or pay that you are not yet able to sustain; the efficiencies are not yet in place to support your profitability. But again, this is rarely the reason your Operating Expenses Account is in the red.

Likewise, some entrepreneurs continue to use their credit cards for day-to-day operations and call them "lines of credit." This is not accurate. It's money you don't have. Your credit card bill is not an expense; it's debt, plain and simple. Using a credit card to cover what you can't afford is also a red flag that your expenses are too high. Stop using the credit card and reserve it for legitimate emergencies or unique circumstances (like for a purchase you must make to yield income).

RAIDING THE TAX ACCOUNT

In the first year or two of doing Profit First, you may get caught in a tax bind because you only pay your estimates. For example, your accountant may prepare estimates based on your business's prior year's income and profitability that say you should make payments of $5000 every quarter.

As your Profit Account and Tax Account grow, you may be surprised to see that you're reserving about $8000 in taxes each quarter. Seeing this, you might think, "Hey, my accountant said I should pay $5000 per quarter. I'm reserving too much for taxes." A little voice inside your head may even say, "Don't touch that money, you'll probably need it for taxes." And then a louder voice will say, "Nah, don't worry about it, you probably won't owe it and even if you do, you have time." Cue the $3000 withdrawal to pay yourself, or pay bills. (A still louder voice—one I've may have heard myself—might say: "Why not start leasing a brand new sports car with that money? Not only is it a business expense, you will instantly become the sexiest beast on this planet." Do not listen! Danger, Will Robinson! Danger!)

Big mistake.

As your profitability grows, your taxes will too. In fact, paying more taxes is an indicator that your business health is improving. Now, I am not saying you should ever pay more taxes than you need to (tax is just an expense like any other), but do realize that your taxes will grow as your business health does. So don't steal from your Tax Account thinking you won't need that money for taxes. You will.

At times, you may even need more than you think. I messed up when I paid my estimated taxes every quarter and then used the extra money to increase my Owner's Pay when I discovered there was money left over. Dummy! Tax estimates are based on your prior year's income. If you make more profit this year (which you will), you will pay more taxes, but your tax *estimates* will not change. If you spend "leftover" money from your Tax Account simply because you allocate more than the estimate, you will be in shock come tax time.

Talk to your PFP every quarter to gauge how you are doing on taxes. And don't take money out of that Tax Account! Your business is growing by leaps and bounds, and higher taxes are definitely in your future.

Another tax issue has to do with paying down debt. I call this "paying for your sins," because if you have debt you need to wipe out, implementing Profit First is going to hurt in the beginning. I should know—it happened to me.

Here's the problem: The government gives you a tax break on expenses but does not consider the money you reserve to pay down debt an expense. The actual charges on your credit card and the interest and credit card fees can be expensed, but not your payments to pay down your cards.

I can't believe I'm saying this, but in this case, the government is right. You get the tax benefit in the year that you make the purchase— no matter if you paid for the expense in cash, by credit card or with funds from a bank loan or line of credit. As you become profitable and pay off debt, you will pay taxes on that income. Eliminating debt and paying taxes will feel like a double whammy. It isn't—you just need to pay for your "sins."

• • •

My own business—and life—has turned around for the better because of Profit First. I am eternally grateful for the financial stability and freedom it has given me. But I also know how easy it is to fall off of the Profit First wagon. It's happened to me, and I've seen it happen to many businesses. Not only do people fall off the wagon, it rolls all over them.

It's easy to fall back into the old ways because they seem to make sense (they don't), or because our accountant says we shouldn't bother (we should), or because we think we were happier doing things the old way (we weren't).

I'll leave you with a quote from the great Sir Roger Bannister, who busted through the myth that the four-minute mile could not be beat: "The man who can drive himself further once the effort gets painful is the man who will win."

Right-o, Sir Roger.

ACTION STEP
GET REAL WITH YOUR ACCOUNTANT

The Only Step: Sit down with your accountant, preferably a PFP trained in this system, and come up with a game plan to ensure that you don't end up allocating too much revenue to your Profit Account and you *do* allocate enough to your Tax Account. Schedule quarterly check-ins to make sure you are consistently building up your profit and other allocations while reducing your operating expenses.

FINANCIAL FREEDOM IS JUST A FEW CLICKS AWAY

12

Life is better on the other side of the street. That's not just a metaphor—I literally live directly across from the house I lived in when my life fell apart due to my own arrogance and belief in top line business principles. And let me tell you, life is much, much better on this side. Not just because we're living in a house that we love. Not just because I took home and kept more salaried income last year than I've ever earned in my life. Life is better because I am no longer a slave to my monthly nut. The Frankenstein monster has become a beautiful Clydesdale workhorse.

Running a Profit First business and lifestyle has given me complete confidence over my finances and freed me from the endless search for a big payout. I'm no longer looking for the Holy Grail—I don't need it. My businesses are profitable today, and they will continue to be profitable tomorrow, next month and in the years to come. I am stringing together small financial win after small financial win— every 10th and 25th of the month.

From my family room window, I can see my old driveway, my old yard, the front door I entered that memorable Valentine's Day when I faced the reality that I'd lost everything. That day, after my daughter slid her piggy bank across the dining room table to me, I stared at it for a few moments, stunned silent. Though the piggy bank was in near-perfect condition, Adayla had secured the bottom stopper with clear sticky tape, duct tape and rubber bands. That's when I remembered a lesson I had long forgotten.

I recalled an earlier conversation when I asked, "Angel, why do you have all that tape over your piggy bank's belly? That stopper works just fine."

She had said, "I'm saving for my own horse, Daddy. Every Sunday when you and Mommy give me my chore money, I run upstairs and put it in here. I don't want it ever coming out, until I have my horse."

That's when it hit me: My nine-year-old daughter had a far better understanding of money management than I did. It was the most humbling moment of my life.

I pushed the piggy bank back to her and said, "Honey, this is yours. We will be fine. I will make sure of it. I will fix what I have broken. But thank you. Thank you from the bottom of my heart."

As low as I felt that day, my daughter's selfless act gave me the courage to let go of my tired ideology and not just recover from my financial problems, but fix them permanently.

The normal response to fixing problems is to try to change our habits. In *The Power of Habit* Charles Duhigg says habits are "click, whirr." Triggered by something (like an empty bank account)—click— we go into our reactionary routine, like making panicky collection calls, for example—whirr. As Duhigg points out in his book, changing habits is possible but is also really, really hard. Instead, simple systems that capture the good parts of our habits and guard us from the bad parts will bring about positive and permanent change, fast.

That's all Profit First is—a simple system that works with us *as we are*. All you have to do is follow it. You don't have to get an MBA, or take an accounting course, or start devouring articles in *The Wall Street Journal*. You don't have to change or "fix" who you are for this to work. It just does.

Why would I ask you to change who you are? You have been able to grow your own, amazing business doing what you do, and that's remarkable by any measure. Now, all we need to do is capture your good money habits and put guard rails up to protect you from your "humanness."

It really is that simple. We are going to put profit first. Period.

You don't need a miracle, or a lucky night in Vegas. You don't need a windfall, or a colossal client, or a worldwide phenomenon to realize the vision you've held for your business since you opened your first box of business cards. You simply need to put your profit first and everything else will fall into line. My daughter, now fifteen, paid her way to Europe with that piggy bank money, and she's close to having enough to buy her horse. It's not rocket science, and you don't have to have a truckload of karma to get it. Financial freedom really is just a few small plates away.

Life *is* better on the other side of the street. Putting your profit first makes it pretty easy to get there.

You know how, at the end of some movies, after the credits roll, there's a little bonus footage? Like in *Ferris Bueller's Day Off*, when Ferris comes back on the screen and says, "You're still here? It's over. Go home. Go."

It's like a little treat for everyone who stayed to watch the credits.

Your bonus for sticking it out, facing the music and slogging through heady content is this:

> If logic worked, everyone would be rich. It's simple—spend less than you make. But you've always known that, and now you know that logic alone doesn't work. Leveraging your emotions and behavior is the most powerful profit-making tool. Profit first. Always.

You're still here? It's over. Go make some money. Go!

ADDITIONAL BOOKS BY MIKE MICHALOWICZ

THE PUMPKIN PLAN

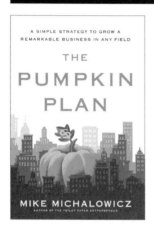

Who would have ever thought that the key to explosive entrepreneurial success was held by pumpkin farmers? Just as almost every pumpkin farmer grows ordinary Halloween carving pumpkins, most entrepreneurs grow ordinary, unremarkable businesses. Yet by tweaking their approach in small ways, farmers can grow giant, prize-winning pumpkins that get all the attention and press coverage. In *The Pumpkin Plan*, Mike Michalowicz—author of the perennial "business cult classic" *The Toilet Paper Entrepreneur*—reveals how applying the same few simple methods farmers use to grow colossal prize-winning pumpkins can lead entrepreneurs to grow colossally successful businesses.

Available at: Amazon.com, Barnesandnoble.com, Audible.com, iTunes.com.

Bulk Purchase (25 or more copies): Joseph Fox Bookshop; (215) 563-4184

THE TOILET PAPER ENTREPRENEUR

It is real. It is raw. It is entrepreneurship. "Never started a company before? Struggling with little or no cash? Have no experience, no baseline to judge your progress against? Thank God! You've got a shot at making this work." So says Mike Michalowicz, author of *The Toilet Paper Entrepreneur*, a business book that is so uniquely useful, so raw and entertaining, it reads like the brainchild of Steve Jobs and Chris Rock. Whether you're just starting out or have been at this for years, Mike's "get real" approach to business is a much needed swift kick in the pants.

Available at: Amazon.com, Audible.com, iTunes.com, MikeMichalowicz.com/Store.

Bulk Purchase (25 or more copies): Offices of Mike Michalowicz; (888) 244-2843 x7002